ACROSS ASIA BY LAND

Adapted by Rachel Kranz from TO THE ENDS OF THE EARTH
by Irene M. Franck and David M. Brownstone

A Volume in the Trade and Travel Routes Series

Facts On File

New York • Oxford

Across Asia by Land

Copyright © 1991 by Irene M. Franck and David M. Brownstone

Facts On File, Inc
460 Park Avenue South
New York NY 10016
USA

Facts On File Limited
Collins Street
Oxford OX4 1XJ
United Kingdom

Library of Congress Cataloging-in-Publication Data

Across Asia by land : adapted from To the ends of the earth by
Irene M. Franck and David M. Brownstone.
    p. cm. — (Trade and travel routes series)
  Includes index.
  Summary: Surveys the history of trade routes in Asia, focusing
especially on the Silk Road from China to the West, but also
including studies of the Ambassador's Road, Burma Road, Eurasian
Steppe Route, and Russian river routes.
  ISBN 0-8160-1874-X
  1. Trade routes—Asia—History—Juvenile literature. 2. Silk
Road—History—Juvenile literature. 3. Asia—Commerce—History—
Juvenile literature. [1. Trade routes—Asia—History. 2. Asia—
Commerce—History.] I. Franck, Irene M. To the ends of the
earth. II. Series.
HE326.A27 1990
380.1'095–dc20   90-37826

A British CIP catalogue record for this book is available from
the British Library.

Facts On File books are available at special discounts when purchased in
bulk quantities for businesses, associations, institutions or sales promotions.
Please call our Special Sales Department in New York at 212/683-2244 (dial
800/322- 8755 except in NY, AK or HI) or in Oxford at 865/728399.

Jacket design by Catherine Hyman
Composition by Facts On File, Inc.
Manufactured by R.R. Donnelly & Sons Company
Printed in the United States of America

10 9 8 7 6 5 4 3 2 1

This book is printed on acid-free paper.

CONTENTS

LIST OF MAPS

PREFACE

Across Asia by Land is one volume in the Travel and Trade Routes series. The series itself is based on our earlier work, *To the Ends of the Earth,* published by Facts On File in 1984. This adaptation of the work for young readers has been prepared by Facts On File; many new illustrations have also been added. The maps, drawn from *To the Ends of the Earth*, are by Dale Adams.

We would also like to acknowledge the permission of several publishers to reprint selections from their works. The excerpts on p. 23–24 are quoted from *The Travels of Fa-Hsien (391–414 A.D.) or Record of the Buddhist Kingdoms*, translated by H.A. Giles and published by Cambridge University Press in 1923. Excerpts on pp. 25–26 are quoted from *Records of the Great Historians of China*, translated from the *Shih Chi* of Ssu-Ma Chien by Burton Watson, © 1961, Columbia University Press. Excerpts on pp. 41, 68–69, 95–96, and 98 are quoted from Ibn Battuta's *Travels, A.D. 1325–1354, translated by H.A.R. Gibb*, published for the Hakluyt Society of Cambridge University Press, 1958–71. The excerpts on pp. 40, 42, 43–44, 67–68, and 94 are from Marco Polo's *The Travels*, translated by Ronald Latham, published by Penguin in 1958, © Ronald Latham, 1958.

Irene M. Franck
David M. Brownstone

INTRODUCTION

WHAT IS A TRADE ROUTE?

In a world without airplanes, engine-powered ships, trucks, or even paved roads, how did people journey from one place to another? How did products that were found only in a very small part of the world eventually find their way to other parts of the world? For almost 5,000 years, people have been trading products from one part of the world to another, using trade routes. Traders from Europe, Asia, and Africa carried furs, spices, silks, pottery, knives, stone utensils, jewels, and a whole host of other commodities, exchanging the products found in one area for the products found in another.

When trading first began, there were no real roads. Local traders might follow trails or cross steep mountain passes in their treks from one village to another. As time passed, tracks might be widened and eventually paved. But the new paved roads tended to follow the old trade routes, establishing these routes as important links of communication between different cultures.

As technology advanced, sea-lanes became vital trade routes between the various continents and made possible trade with North America, South America, and Australia. The many ways in which the highways and seaways have been used for trade over the years have shaped the course of history.

WHY STUDY TRADE ROUTES?

Studying the trade routes of the world is one way of learning about the history of the world. As we look at the trade routes of Europe, for example, we can see how the nations of that continent have changed throughout the centuries: we learn how Scandinavian Vikings came to sail south and west to settle in France and Britain; we can appreciate how present-day Hungary was originally settled by a wandering tribe from the Ural Mountains, and so on. In a similar way, by looking at the trade routes of Africa, we can trace the history of the slave trade and learn about the European colonization of Africa in the 18th and 19th centuries.

In addition, studying the trade routes helps us better understand the origin of many of the institutions and services with which we are familiar today. Postal systems, tolls, guidebooks, roadside restaurants and hotels all came into being either to serve or because of trade routes. Studying the trade routes will help you to understand how they emerged.

HOW TO USE THIS BOOK

This book is organized in chapters. Each chapter is devoted to the history of one trade route or, in some cases, where the particular trade route has an especially long and eventful history, to a particular era in a trade route's history. Therefore, you can simply read about one trade route that particularly interests you or, alternatively, read about all the trade routes in a given area. After the discussion of each route, you will find a list of books for further reading, which will assist you in locating additional resources should you need them to support report research or classroom work. If you are using this book as a reference for a particular history course, check the index to find the subject or person you need to know more about. The list of maps at the front of this book will direct you to all maps contained herein, and thereby help you to locate each trade route on the face of the globe.

Studying trade routes can be a fascinating way of learning about world history—and of understanding more about our lives today. We hope you enjoy all the volumes in the Trade and Travel Routes series.

ACROSS ASIA
BY LAND

1

THE SILK ROAD: CHINA'S EARLY DAYS

THE SILK ROAD: LINKING THE PEOPLES OF WEST AND EAST

One of the longest trade routes in the world was the Silk Road of China. This immense road stretched 5,000 miles, from east Asia all the way to the Mediterranean Sea. For thousands of years the Silk Road linked the peoples of the East with those of the West.

Many different types of goods traveled along the Silk Road. But the most famous was the one that gave the route its name—silk. This precious material was made in China and was prized by Europeans who traded gold and other valuable goods for it. To trade for silk, Europeans endured dangerous journeys that lasted months or even years, crossing burning deserts and icy mountains.

Besides silk, Europeans were eager for Chinese porcelain (fine dishes, or "china"), ornaments, jewelry, and other products. Western nations that wanted these goods sent explorers (such as Marco Polo) eastward, looking for land and sea routes that would facilitate trade.

The Silk Road was not used only by traders. Because the Silk Road passed through many different nations, armies often used it on campaigns. Priests and religious travelers carried the ideas of Buddhism, an Indian religion, from India into China. And diplomats used the road to forge alliances between the different nations along the route.

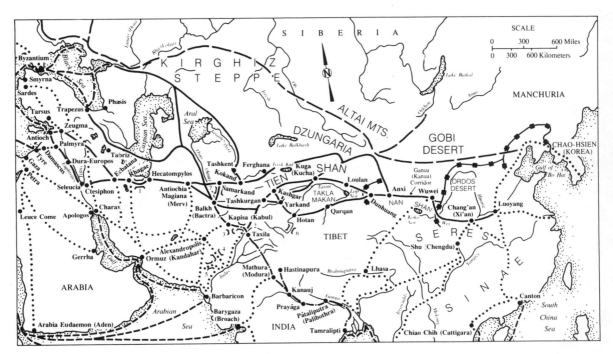

The Silk Road and Other Eurasian Routes in Greco-Roman Times

——— Main Silk Routes
—·—·— Indian Grand Road
— — — Eurasian Steppe Route
········· Main Connecting Land Routes
- - - - - Main Connecting Sea Routes
—■—■— Fortified Wall

⊨ Passes:
1. Caspian Gates
2. Khyber Pass
3. Kurram Pass
4. Bolan Pass
5. Mula Pass
6. Karakorum Pass
7. Iron Gates

The Silk Road and China's History. Although the Silk Road was used by many different peoples and empires for thousands of years, its story is in many ways the story of China.

During some periods the Chinese welcomed trade and contact with other nations. In fact, they might even expand and conquer other peoples to try to widen their own territory.

During other periods, however, the Chinese pulled back inside their borders and discouraged contact with the outside world. The Great Wall of China—a huge, impressive wall snaking many thousands of miles across northern China—was built to protect the Chinese from northern invaders. But the wall also served as a symbol to both China and other nations, saying, "We will stay inside our borders, and you stay inside yours."

Sometimes the Chinese held both of these positions at the same time. In the 19th century, for example, they could not avoid trading with the Europeans, as they feared coercion if they refused. Therefore, the Chinese continued their trade with outsiders—but they did everything they could to prevent contact with them. In an attempt to stem the flow of European ideas through China, Europeans were only allowed to live in certain parts of the trading cities.

This chapter will survey the history of the Silk Road up to the seventh century A.D.

THE SILK ROAD'S ROUTE

The Silk Road ran through some of the world's most treacherous territory. Because of changing political systems, national boundaries, weather conditions, and geography, this trade route has varied over the past 3,000 years.

The Eastern Half of the Silk Road. The Silk Road began in northern China. This eastern end of the Silk Road changed over the centuries. In early times it was generally located at either Chang'an (near the modern city of Xi'an) or Luoyang (Loyang). Later the Silk Road began in the more modern capital city of Beijing.

Out in the Central Asian desert, sandstorms were a real hazard, for they could suffocate travelers who did not cover their faces—and might even bury a whole caravan. (By Sven Hedin, from his *Through Asia, 1899*)

From here the Silk Road headed west, along the Gansu (Kansu) Corridor, which runs between the Gobi Desert to the north and the Nan Shan (Southern Mountains) to the south. When the earliest form of the Great Wall of China was built—around the third century B.C.—it protected the northern side of the Silk Road.

The Silk Road left the Great Wall's protection when it passed through Yumen, which is also known as the Jade Gate. Here the Silk Road entered Central Asia. It passed through the salt flats (a marshy area with salt water) around the swamplike lake called the Lop Nor. At this point, the Silk Road encountered a large natural obstacle: the Takla Makan Desert. This is one of the most bleak and unwelcoming places in the world. Many deserts are relatively full of life—cacti, palm trees, lizards, rabbits—but very little lives in the Takla Makan Desert. It is made of vast waves of shifting sand dunes that, in sudden storms, might easily bury a caravan—or even a whole town.

For thousands of years this desert struck terror into the hearts of travelers. Newcomers were always warned not to stray from the main path and also warned against the mirages (illusions) and imaginary sounds of the desert. Travelers would "see" a mirage or "hear" a noise and be lured off the path into the dangerous sand dunes.

To avoid these dangers, the Silk Road turned away from the desert. Over the years travelers found two routes around it.

The Southern Way followed the foothills of the Kunlun Mountains through the oases of Qarqan (now Quiemo) and Hotan (Khotan) all the way to the city of Yarkand (Schache). This was the first route travelers found, and it led them to the Hotan jade market. (Jade is a green or white stone that is highly valued for use in jewelry and other ornaments.) However, the Southern Way was very dry, with little food or water. This prompted travelers to discover the Northern Way. This route followed the Tien Shan (Celestial Mountains) through the oases of Louland and Kuga (Kucha). It ended in either Yarkand or Kashgar (Kashi). The Northern Way was watered by streams and had better grazing for the horses, oxen, or cattle that travelers might be taking with them. However, the Northern Way was open to raids by the peoples of the north.

The Western Half of the Silk Road. At Yarkand and Kashgar, travelers faced the Pamir mountain range, a high, crumpled plateau that stretched 300 miles to the west. This was hard traveling, too, but of a different kind. Many of the Pamir passes were narrow and dangerous. In addition, the air of high mountain altitudes doesn't have as much oxygen as does air lower down. So travelers in the Pamir often suffered from dizziness, headaches, and ringing ears. The Persians (an ancient people, ancestors of today's Iranians) called this rugged country the "Roof of the World."

On the other side of the Pamir, travelers headed for the city of Bactra (Balkh). This lovely city, about halfway along the Silk Road, was known to many as "paradise on earth." It is set in a beautiful and fertile valley, in what is currently the northern part of Afghanistan.

Bactra stood at the intersection of two great trade routes, China's Silk Road and India's Grand Road. In fact, it was the northernmost point of the Grand Road.

From Bactra, the Silk Road headed west through the town of Merv and then up onto the Iranian Plateau, which is the area where modern-day Iran is located. The route continued south of the Caspian Sea, where it reached the great cities of Rhagae (Rayy, near Iran's modern capital city of Tehran) and Ecbatana (Hamadan).

As the Silk Road continued west, it passed through the ancient country of Mesopotamia (in the modern country of Iraq). Going farther west, it reached great ancient cities, such as Babylon, Seleucia, and Baghdad (which still exists as the modern capital of Iraq).

Finally, the Silk Road turned northward toward Antioch, in Syria. That was the western end of the Silk Road. From Antioch, goods

In the high, very dry valleys leading to Balkh, camel caravans still follow the line of the old Silk Road. (Delia and Ferdinand Kuhn)

from the East were shipped across the Mediterranean Sea, where they finally reached European cities, such as Rome.

Alternate Routes. In some places routes would branch off from the main Silk Road to the south, north, or west. A certain city or region might become important for a century or two, causing travelers to find their way to do it. Or perhaps war, drought, or other disturbances made it necessary to avoid certain portions of the old Silk Road. However, the basic span of the Silk Road was from Beijing to Antioch—a 5,000-mile journey across the continent of Asia.

EARLY TIMES

Nomads. In the region spanned by the Silk Road, the first movement across the vast distances seems to have begun with the nomadic peoples of Central Asia. *Nomads*, or wanderers, are people who don't live in any one place. They live for a while in one area, building huts or setting up tents for shelter, and then move on to another area. They might be hunters, or they might graze flocks of cattle, oxen, camels, or sheep. Before they wear out the resources of an area—before they hunt too many animals or graze too much grass—they move on to somewhere else.

Several centuries before the birth of Christ, the peoples of Central Asia seem to have migrated northward in summer, to the higher, cooler plains. Then, in winter, they would move south, where it was warmer. They carried with them some valuable items and traded these items with each other.

This trade was one of the first ways that peoples of different regions began to learn about others who lived elsewhere and to understand that different regions had different resources. The ancient territory of Mesopotamia received gold, tin, and turquoise from the Iranian plateau; lapis lazuli (a beautiful blue stone used as a jewel) and rubies from Afghanistan; and cotton cloth from India—all because of these nomadic peoples.

China also traded with the nomads. At this point in its history, China's borders did not stretch halfway across Asia; the old China began as a settlement of many different peoples far to the east, in the Wei and Huang valleys. To this settlement came goods from far across the continent: Iranian turquoise, Afghan lapis lazuli, gold from Siberia, and jade from Hotan (which at this time was not part of China).

The nomads tamed horses so that they could ride from place to place. In addition, they tamed the two-hump Bactran camel. These beasts not only carried people—they carried goods for people to trade.

Nomads Transmitting New Ideas. Goods weren't the only thing to travel in this early trade. Ideas and new ways of doing things were also carried back and forth. Imagine a time when no one had ever heard of the wheel, when no one had ever thought that language could be written down. Then imagine the nomads of Central Asia circulating these ideas around the continent. They also brought the idea of the chariot (a cart that rode on two wheels and could be pulled by a horse) and new ways of working with metal.

The nomads didn't carry just peaceful ideas. They also helped spread new ideas about war. By 1500 B.C., soldiers fought in chariots, which allowed them to move much more quickly than on foot. Between 1500 B.C. and 500 B.C., Central Asian soldiers began to fight on horseback, which gave them even more freedom of movement and made it easier to get closer to an enemy. The Iranians seem to have been the first people to come up with this idea, which made them powerful forces. But the practice of mounted warfare (or *cavalry*, as it is called) soon spread to China and the West as well.

Although these nomads were so important to the ancient countries they traveled between, we really know very little about them. Scholars have looked at historical records to get more information— but because every country had its own name for these people, we don't always know exactly who is being talked about or whether they are the same people. Additionally, the countries of China and Mesopotamia were so far away from each other that for most of the thousand years before Christ, they didn't really even know that the other country existed. All they knew were that nomads had brought them trade goods and rumors from someplace very far away.

The First Exploration of Central Asia. Both the Chinese and the Mesopotamians became very curious about the other country that they did so much trade with. But which country was the first to explore Central Asia in order to find out more? We don't really know the answer to that. There is, however, a Chinese legend on the subject. According to the Chinese story, Princess Hsi Wang Mu lived in the West and was visited by Chinese Emperor Mu-Wang in about 1000 B.C. Mu-Wang's travel memoirs tell how the "God of the river" showed him "the precious articles of the Ch-un Mountain," including gems and valuable jade. Perhaps Chinese explorers did reach the jade markets of Hotan during these early centuries—but there is no evidence to prove the case.

China Builds a Great Wall. The Chinese were interested in pushing westward. At this time, China was ruled by the Ch'in dynasty (221–207 B.C.). This dynasty had unified many different peoples to form one of the first versions of China—a small country located in the Wei Valley in the Far East. But this unified country was always under attack from nomads of the desert steppes to the north and the west.

The Chinese decided to protect themselves by building fortifications against invaders. By the third century B.C., these fortifications had been joined to form a Great Wall.

Today the Great Wall is a "long stone serpent" that snakes across the northern part of China. In those early days, however, the wall was built from dirt and wattles (sticks woven together). It stretched all the way from Korea around the Gulf of Bo Hai, across the northern Huang River, and down its western bank. The Great Wall was staffed by soldiers—who were often criminals sent out to serve on China's farthest frontiers. These soldiers would light signal fires at the first sign of invaders.

New Invaders. Initially, the Great Wall was successful at keeping invaders out. But the Chinese army became weaker as it faced a new and very serious threat from the northern steppes. The Chinese called these people the Hsiung-nu. The Europeans called them the Huns.

When the Hsiung-nu moved down from the north, they pushed out an earlier invading people, the Yueh-chih, which the Europeans knew as the Scythians. The Hsiung-nu had pushed the Yueh-chih all the way west, to the Black Sea. So the Chinese thought that they might welcome an alliance against the Hsiung-nu. Under the Emperor Wu-Ti, an expedition was sent to try to form one.

CHANG CH'IEN'S LONG TRIP WEST

In 138 B.C. a party of 100 men left for the West, led by the great Chinese explorer Chang Ch'ien, to make an alliance with the Yueh-chih against the Hsiung-nu. But the trip would also become a way for the Chinese to understand far more about the people to their west.

Chang Ch'ien's trip was not easy. At first he and his men were captured by the Hsiung-nu and were kept as prisoners for 10 years. Finally they were able to escape.

Chang Ch'ien and his men followed a line of oases through the jade country of Hotan. They arrived on the other side of the Takla Makan Desert, in what was then the land of Ferghana (Ta-yuan), along the upper part of the Jaxartes River. Today that area is part of China, but 2,100 years ago it was a separate country. The king of Ferghana had heard of the wealth of China and wanted to establish communication with the country to his north. He helped Chang Ch'ien by giving him guides and interpreters for the rest of his trip.

But the Yueh-Chih were not interested in an alliance. They had been pushed to the west, all the way to the region of Bactra, in the modern-day country of Iran. They were secure and successful in their new homeland and not interested in fighting the Hsiung-nu. After waiting for a whole year in the hope of changing their minds, Chang Ch'ien left for home—but was captured by the Hsiung-nu once more! Once again he escaped. When he finally arrived back in China in 126 B.C., he was with his wife (whom he had married during the period of his first captivity), a servant—and only two of the original group he had started out with 12 long years before.

A New Kind of Horse. Chang Ch'ien's mission had failed in its primary objective, but his trip was a success in another way. He had found out that the eager traders of Ferghana had powerful horses "which sweat blood; their forebears are supposed to have been foaled [born] from heavenly horses." Of course, the horses did not really "sweat blood"—they were affected by parasites that caused bleeding sores. But that did not seem to hurt the horses.

These new, powerful horses were far better than the small Chinese ponies for mounted warfare. Their hooves were especially hardy and difficult to wear down. These were the days before horseshoes were used to protect horses' hooves, so hard hooves were important.

Word of Other Lands. Another important result of Chang Ch'ien's trip was the information he carried about countries beyond Bactra. Although he had not seen these lands himself, he brought back to China the first stories of them. Beyond Bactra was An-hsi (Persia, also part of today's Iran). West of that was T'iao-chih, or Syria, "near the western sea"—that is, the Mediterranean. According to Chang Ch'ien's report, the "old men of An-hsi" said that the

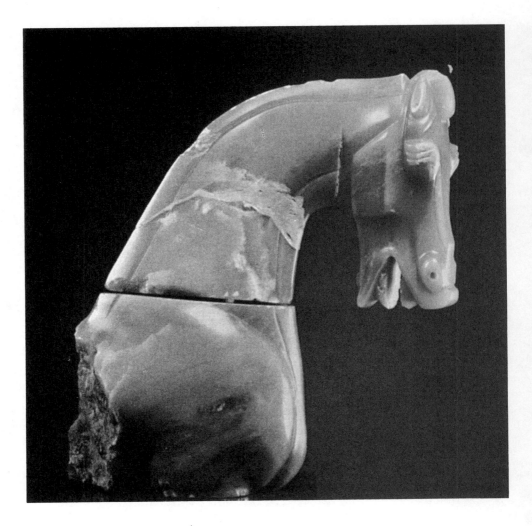

This is one of the fine horses of Ferghana, carved in the jade so much prized by the Chinese. (Han period, from the Victoria and Albert Museum)

mythical princess of Hsi Wang Mu lived in T'iao-chih. That shows that the ancient legend of the Chinese princess who traveled west was still alive.

Chang Ch'ien also reported that "to the north of An-hsi there lies a country called Li-chien." The explorer seems to have known only the name of this northern country. But that was China's first knowledge of the Roman Empire, the powerful European empire that spread out from the Italian city of Rome. Soon after Chang Ch'ien's journey, Rome and China would become important trading partners.

Another country that the Chinese learned about from this trip was called Shen-tu—India. The Chinese were interested in trading with this country, too, but were discouraged by the jungles and Tibetan mountains that lay in the way.

Chang Ch'ien's Second Trip. Less than 10 years after his first journey ended, Chang Ch'ien embarked on a second journey. This time he wanted to form an alliance with the Wu-sun, a Central Asian people. Although the Wu-sun were skeptical at first, they eventually decided to trade with China. Soon many states to the northwest began to trade with China. These new international relations were all due to Chang Ch'ien. His trips opened the way for good relations between China and its neighbors, and it was his good reputation that helped these neighboring lands welcome the other Chinese ambassadors that came after him.

Chang Ch'ien's journeys were important for bringing in a new period of Chinese trade.

New Chinese Trade

China was eventually successful in defeating the Hsiung-nu, and the Chinese drove them far north, to Central Asia (the part of the world that today is Mongolia). In this way, the Chinese themselves expanded their power all the way to the Jaxartes River. Slowly but surely, the Chinese were developing an east–west trade route that would eventually form the basis of the Silk Road.

China Fights with Kokand. Relations between China and its trading partners were not always smooth. The Chinese depended on other peoples to supply their needs over the long east–west route, and very often these peoples were not so helpful.

The Chinese also did not always get everything they wanted in their trading deals. Once the Chinese strongly desired some horses from a village near Kokand, in the Central Asian region that is now part of Uzbekistan, one of the Asian republics of the Soviet Union. The Chinese sent "a great quantity of silver and a horse made of solid gold" to pay for the horses. But the Kokand rulers decided that they already had enough Chinese silver and gold and refused to send the horses. They thought they could do so safely, because China was so far off and the journey so difficult that no army could ever reach them.

They were wrong. The Chinese put together tens of thousands of soldiers and great stores of supplies. Then they marched across

To get battle horses like this one, the Chinese traveled halfway across Asia. (T'ang bas-relief, University Museum, Pennsylvania)

Central Asia to lay siege to Kokand. When the Chinese cut off Kokand's water supply, the city finally surrendered.

The war also proved costly to the Chinese. Only one-sixth of the army returned. They tried to bring back 3,000 horses with them, but 2,000 were lost along the way. Through careful breeding, however, the Chinese used the remaining 1,000 horses to create a new breed of war-horse.

Once the Chinese had gotten these horses, they decided that they needed very little else from the outside world. They imported some precious metals and jewels but were generally becoming more isolated. No longer did they welcome strangers or move much beyond their own boundaries.

CHINA'S NEW FOREIGN RELATIONS

China and Parthia. The Chinese did continue to maintain some foreign relations. After Chang Ch'ien's famous journeys, other ambassadors went west. One went to Parthia, an ancient kingdom, southeast of the Caspian Sea, which is located in the country that is today's Iraq. This ambassador was met at the border by a huge

escort that included 20,000 horses. When the Chinese ambassador finally returned home, he brought with him a Parthian ambassador, who presented to the Chinese court an ostrich egg and some magicians from the Roman Empire, Parthia's western neighbor.

Parthia was eventually absorbed into the Persian Empire, and these meetings, which took place from about 115 to 105 B.C., formed the tentative beginnings of Chinese-Persia trade relations.

Parthian warriors like these defeated the Romans and took firm control of the Iranian portion of the Silk Road. (Royal Ontario Museum)

China and Rome. Soon after the meetings between the Chinese and the Parthians, Chinese goods reached farther west. But interestingly, it took a war to carry them there. In 53 B.C. the Romans fought the Parthians at Carrhae, near the Euphrates River (in today's Iraq). At a key point in the battle, the Parthians unfurled their brilliantly colored banners of shining silk. This was the first time that the Romans had seen the dazzling material, and they were impressed. Later the Romans would seek to trade with the Chinese themselves.

China in Central Asia. The Chinese began to expand their borders even farther. Now that they had driven the Hsiung-nu north, they took Central Asia territories into their empire. They guarded these territories with forts staffed by Chinese soldiers. Most of these soldiers were convicts and exiles who had no choice but to serve as commanded. By the middle of the first century A.D., the Chinese were fully in control of the Silk Road west to the Jaxartes River.

Mountain travelers often had to travel on dangerous "trestle roads," wooden balconies built out from cliffsides, as here near the China–Tibet border. (From Cooper, *Travels of a Pioneer of Commerce*, reprinted in H. Yule and H. Cordier, *The Book of Ser Marco Polo*, 1903)

China, Rome, and Persia. By 29 B.C. the Roman emperor Caesar Augustus had brought peace to his empire. There were no more civil wars from that time on. In addition, the Roman wars with the Persians, a people who had established a large empire along the Persian Gulf, had reached a stalemate. Neither side had won—but they were no longer actively fighting. Instead, they agreed upon a border in Mesopotamia.

However, the Persians would not permit any foreigners to pass through their territory and insisted that they act as middlemen in any east–west trade in which Rome was interested.

The Romans didn't like this and tried to develop a northern route around Persia, but they failed. They did find a sea route that went east, which eventually became the basis of the Spice Route. However, the Romans had to depend on the Persians for an east–west land route.

SILK AND THE WEST

Once the Persians got hold of Chinese silk, how was this precious good transported farther west? The journey began with traders who brought the cloth down into Mesopotamia. From there it either went directly to the Romans at Antioch in Syria or though the city of Palmyra in the Syrian desert.

At this point, the silk was still "raw." It had not been woven into the soft and shiny fabric that was so precious. Instead, it looked more like rough cotton and was a natural color. The raw silk went to seaside towns on the banks of the Mediterranean, where it was dyed. A people called the Phoenicians, who then lived in the territory that today is the country of Lebanon, had a famous purple dye that was often used on silk. This Phoenician purple was so precious that, for many years, only royalty and senior members of government could wear it. That's where the expression "royal purple" comes from.

The term "Phoenician royal purple" was used to describe many different shades of violet. This color could range from what we call red down to a dark blue-violet that was almost black. To do their work, the dyers required freshly killed shellfish, so they worked only in sea-side towns during autumn and winter, when shellfish were plentiful.

At first, Chinese silk was so expensive and rare that the Romans wore it only in patches or stripes on their basic white tunics. They usually preferred purple or gold silk. Under some rulers, anyone wearing "royal purple" who wasn't royalty could be put to death.

Over many years the Romans became used to having silk. Then, in the first century A.D., the Chinese became embroiled in civil war. The overland Silk Road was barely used, and the supply of silk was nearly cut off. The fabric became extremely rare in the West. Only a little silk reached the Romans, coming by way of India, by sea, on the Spice Route.

THE FOUR POWERS

By late in the first century A.D., the Chinese had restored order and reopened their trade routes to the West. But when they came back into contact with the rest of the world, they discovered that they had been joined by another power in Central Asia—the Kushans. The Kushans' kingdom was formed of Yueh-chih (Scythians) and Indo-Greeks. These last were Greek descendants of Alexander the Great's army who had settled in India.

The Kushans were a strong new force on the Silk Road. Their power stretched from the western oases of the Takla Makan Desert south into the Indus River valley, in India; north to the Aral Sea, which today is in the Soviet Asian republics of Kazakhstan and Uzbekistan. The heartland of the Kushans was in Sogdiana, between the Oxus and Jaxartes rivers.

With the rise of the Kushans, there were four great powers along the 5,000-mile Silk Road—the Chinese, the Kushans, the Persians, and the Romans. This was the first great period of the Silk Road: the route was now fully developed and a busy trade thoroughfare. At this point, the route was divided into sections, with goods being carried in turn by Chinese, Kushan, Persian, and Roman caravans.

THE CARAVAN TRADE

The Silk Road was peaceful for a time during the first century A.D. with the four main powers keeping the way secure. Silk Road caravans—groups of people and animals traveling together over long desert distances—followed an established route. They began in Chang'an in northern China, or else in Luoyang in southern China. Wherever they started, they made their way west through the Jade Gate, in Yumen.

Beyond the Jade Gate was the three-to-four-week trip to the Lop Nor, the dry swampy salt lake of Central Asia. On one side of the Lop Nor were the Hsiung-nu; on the other side were the Tibetans. Both peoples threatened the caravans. So did the wild camels of the region. If a caravan survived, it would move on past the drifting red-gold sand dunes of the Taklan Makan Desert to the main oasis of Hotan.

Caravan Life. One of the chief problems of caravan life was finding drinkable water for both people and animals. Another was sticking to the trail, which could sometimes be covered by a sudden sandstorm. In summer the sun was so hot that caravans often had to travel by night. Some caravan pilots trained at a school for sailors in India, so that at night they could navigate by the stars, like ships' pilots.

Caravan travelers usually camped out in the open, with only tents to shield them from the cold night air—or from the hot daytime sun. When a caravan arrived at an oasis, it often rested for a few days or even weeks. This was also a time for repairing caravan equipment. Traders would exchange some of their goods for local products, then exchange those for other goods farther down the trail.

For safety, caravans sometimes joined together so that as many as 1,000 camels might be traveling together. Archers were also hired to protect caravans from robbers who might attack them along the way.

Another obstacle on the caravan route was the Pamir Mountains, which had deep river gorges, steep passes, and high meadows. The high mountain air has less oxygen than lowland air and causes both humans and animals to suffer from altitude sickness.

On the eastern part of the route, caravans depended mainly on horses and camels. In the rougher mountain sections, however, mules and yaks were preferred. These animals often gave warnings of danger, which wise guides watched out for. The Chinese book *Pei Shih* describes how camels might sometimes alert travelers to a dangerous sandstorm in the Takla Makan Desert:

> When such a wind is about to arrive, only the old camels have advance knowledge of it, and they immediately stand snarling together, and bury their mouths in the sand. The men always take this as a sign, and they too immediately cover their noses and mouths by wrapping them in felt. This wind moves swiftly, and passes in a moment, and is gone, but if they did not so protect themselves, they would be in danger of sudden death.

Once the caravans had crossed the Pamirs, they made their way to the Stone Tower, on the Yarkand River. The Stone Tower was the central meeting place for merchants of China, India, Persia, and Bactra. Because these traders all spoke different languages, they had either to hire interpreters or find creative ways to communicate.

From there, goods went in several directions. Some went north. More went through Bactra to India, in the south. Most went through Persia to Mesopotamia. There, the Persians traded with the Greek, Syrian, and Jewish merchants who would bring eastern goods farther west, to Rome. These merchants used the Great Desert

Within the mountains, local trade has always focused on the caravan stops, where goods are exchanged, here rice for wool. (Delia and Ferdinand Kuhn)

Route to cross through the Middle East, and there one-humped camels, known as dromedaries, carried the traders and their goods.

The Economics of Trade. It was very expensive to carry goods over the thousands of miles of the Silk Road. To justify the high expenses that were incurred, goods had to be lightweight, easily carried, and very valuable. That way a merchant could make a considerable profit on the goods that only one camel could carry, rather than spending more money on more camels to carry heavier and cheaper products.

Silk fitted the bill perfectly, as it was both light and expensive, and there was a large market for it—the Romans. They bought so much silk that in the first century A.D., the Roman emperor Tiberius passed a law forbidding men to wear silk. The story was that Tiberius feared that silk would weaken the Romans, but probably he wanted to reduce the amount of Roman gold flowing east.

China preferred to receive gold in exchange for its goods. But it was also attracted by perfumes and cosmetics from Egypt, Arabia, and Persia, and by finely made jewelry and colored glass from Syria

So much gold was spent in buying silks like those worn here that, in the first century A.D., the Romans passed a law forbidding men to wear silk. ("House of the Tragic Poet —Sallust," from L. W. Yaggy and T. L. Haines, *Museum of Antiquity*, 1882)

and Mesopotamia. The nomads of the Eurasian steppes—the part of the world that is now in the Soviet Union, between Europe and Asia—also had a taste for silk. These nomads added furs and human slaves to the mix of things traded along the great Silk Road.

BUDDHIST MISSIONARIES

At first, most long-distance travelers on the Silk Road were traders, soldiers, or diplomats. But in the first century A.D., during the time of the Kushans, missionaries from India joined these travelers. The missionaries were carrying the old Indian religion of Buddhism into China and Central Asia.

The Buddhist missionaries from India traveled on the main roads as well as on the rough tracks and trails of the high Himalayan Mountains. Buddhism followed the Silk Road from Hotan into China and quickly spread through those trading centers that had large foreign populations. It spread north to the Hsiung-nu and south below the Yangtze River. By the middle of the second century

A.D., Luoyang had become a prime center for translating Buddhist works into Chinese.

THE END OF AN ERA

Changes in the West. By the third century A.D., the balance of power along the Silk Road had begun to shift. In the West, the Roman Empire had already split into two parts. The Western Roman Empire had become a Christian nation whose church was the Catholic Church and whose spiritual leader was the Pope, in Rome. The Eastern Roman Empire was centered in the city of Constantinople (now called Istanbul, in the modern country of Turkey). Its church was the Eastern Orthodox Church, another branch of Christianity, and its spiritual leader was the Patriarch. This empire covered Greece and parts of the Middle East, including areas in what today are the countries of Turkey, Lebanon, and Syria.

By this time, the Western Roman Empire had begun to weaken. The Eastern Roman Empire—later called the Byzantine Empire—became the new center of the Roman world. Along with Antioch, the

Silk Road traders are met by a Turkish chief on the shores of the Caspian Sea. (19th century, authors' archives)

Byzantine capital of Constantinople became one of the main western destinations of the Silk Road.

Persia also went through many political upheavals. A new people came to rule it. These new leaders were able to take over large pieces of Kushan territory.

Invaders. During the third through the sixth or seventh centuries A.D., new waves of invaders from the northern steppes attacked both the Kushans and the Chinese. These nomadic peoples came down into Europe and Asia and contributed greatly to the turbulence of European history.

In China, too, the northern invaders contributed to the breakup of the empire. Up to this point, the Han had ruled China. A series of weak governments replaced their empire. The Hsiung-nu continued to move down from the north, and eventually they moved so far south that they cut the Silk Road. For a time, caravans no longer traveled the Silk Road.

The arresting of travel on the Silk Road was a sore blow to both Rome and China, for both empires depended on the trade conducted over this route. Furthermore, this began an period where the two nations had little or no direct contact with each other. Over the centuries each would develop strange myths about the former trading partner.

Persia was less upset at the loss of the Silk Road, for it now controlled the Spice Route, the sea-lane that linked east and west. Some east–west trade did continue by sea, but land travel ceased.

The invaders brought an end to an era in more ways than one. They made farming impossible in many Central Asian oases, for they burned cities and drove farmers away. These farmers had once grown food for caravan travelers. Now, even if travel had been safe, it would have been much more difficult. Eventually, nature finished what the invaders started. Over the centuries the whole central region of China became much drier and farming would have been impossible in any case.

New Routes for the Silk Road. During this period starting in the third century A.D., the Chinese found other routes that passed farther north. One route curved northwest through Turfan before rejoining the old route through Kuga. This new route was more attractive than the old path through the salt flats, as we can tell from its Chinese name: the Road Through the Willows.

Later, when the area became more peaceful, travelers took a route that was even farther north. They passed through the Khirgiz

Steppe (now the Kirghiz Republic of the Soviet Union), toward Tashkent (now capital of the Uzbekistan Republic of the Soviet Union) or Samarkand (also in the Uzbekistan Soviet Republic).

Central Asia traders tried out many different routes to Constantinople, because the Byzantines in that city were eager to trade in silk. Because so much silk had to pass through Persia, that country still had a monopoly on silk—but both the Central Asians and the Byzantines were eager to compete. The fact that the West's demand for silk was increasing added to the competition. The Christian churches, especially, liked to use silk for the robes of their officials.

The Secret of Silk-Making. For many centuries China continued to keep the process of silk-making a secret, which meant that anybody who wanted to trade in silk had to deal with the Chinese. But in the fifth century, this secret began to leak out. Exactly how this happened is unclear. Many stories have been told to explain it, but we aren't certain how true they are.

Some stories tell of a Chinese princess who brought the secret to her bridegroom, the king of Hotan (a city that was not yet part of China). According to this story, the princess carried the silkworms—the insects that spin silk threads—inside her wig. Because all Chinese women, even the nobles, learned how to produced silk, she would have known how to turn the silkworms' threads into silk. Silkworms eat mulberry leaves—and, this story says, somehow the king of Hotan managed to find mulberry trees on which the silkworms could feed.

In the sixth century, Constantinople received the secret of silk-making. Supposedly some monks traveling west carried some silkworms with them, hidden in a hollow cane. In the same period, Persia, too, finally learned how to make silk. However, Hotan, Constantinople, and Persia did not manage to capitalize on their knowledge. Their silk was of poor quality, whereas China's silk was excellent. Demand for the better-quality silk continued for many centuries to come.

China's New Skills. At about the same time, the Chinese learned how to make the special colored glass that they had originally traded for from the West. In the early seventh century they also learned how to make porcelain—the fine material for dishes that became a Chinese specialty. As a result of their new skills, the Chinese lost interest in the western colored glass and pottery that they had prized before. Once again China had reduced its need for contact with the outside world.

BUDDHIST PILGRIMS

During the centuries of China's isolation, few people crossed China's borders in either direction. The only exceptions were the brave Buddhist pilgrims who made their way—often on foot and alone— across Central Asia into India. They left China to find and bring back copies of religious texts. Because Buddhism had begun in India, Chinese Buddhists felt strongly the need to communicate with their fellow Buddhists in India.

Many pilgrims took years to make their journeys. They often stopped at monasteries along the way. A pilgrim might spend months or even years at a monastery, studying the religious texts there and learning more about his religion. To honor the monks, special religious meetings were often held. The Chinese pilgrim Fa-Hsien writes of one religious gathering held in Kashgar in the fifth century A.D.:

> ...[the King] invites Shamans [Buddhists] from all quarters, and these collect together like clouds. The place where the priests are to sit is splendidly adorned beforehand with streaming pennants and canopies of silk; silk embroidered with lotus flowers in gold and silver, is also laid over the backs of seats. When all is in order, the king and his ministers make their offerings according to rite [religious ceremony]...

Hsuan Tsang. One of the best known of the Chinese Buddhist pilgrims was Hsuan Tsang. In the early seventh century he decided to travel to other Buddhist countries in order to question the wise people there on religious points that he wanted to resolve. His journey was a difficult and dramatic adventure.

When Hsuan Tsang made his journey, there was a ban against travel. Nevertheless, he stole past the watchtowers that guarded the exits out of China toward the west. Sometimes he was caught by guards for the Chinese government—but many of these were Buddhist, and Hsuan Tsang played on their religious feelings to win their sympathy.

Then, without companions or guide, Hsuan Tsang set out with only vague directions for the nearest waterhole. Almost immediately he dropped his waterbag, spilling all of the precious water that he needed to make his long desert journey. Hardly knowing where he was going or where to find more water, he stumbled on.

In the end, it was Hsuan Tsang's horse who saved him. The horse could smell the scent of green pastures blown upon the wind. It led both of them to the water they needed.

Somehow, Hsuan Tsang made his way to Turfan. Today Turfan is a Chinese city, but in those days it was controlled by Turkey—the land whose capital was then Constantinople.

Then Hsuan Tsang needed a promise of safe passage from the Turkish leader. To get it, he threaded his way through the mountains called Tien Shan (again, part of China today, but

This rather unflattering portrait of Hsuan Tsang, complete with sandals and backpack, was found in the Cave of the Thousand Buddhas in Dunhuang. (Stein Collection, British Museum)

not then). Here's how Hsuan Tsang described those difficult mountains:

> From the beginning of the world the snow had accumulated [here]…and has turned into blocks of ice, which melt neither in springtime nor in summer. They roll away in boundless sheets of hard, gleaming white, losing themselves in the clouds…

Finally Hsuan Tsang reached India. For 15 years he crisscrossed the holy trails of that land, before he finally headed homeward again. For his return trip, he chose to traverse the immense mountain range called the Hindu Kush, which he called the Snowy Mountains.

That route proved to be very hard. This is what he wrote about the highest mountain on this route: "So high was this peak that the frozen clouds and the wind-driven snow did not even reach its peak." After the Kush came the dizzying Pamir mountains. And in both mountain ranges Hsuan Tsang and the small caravan of travelers he had joined had to be ever on their guard against robbers.

In the end, though, Hsuan Tsang survived the mountain journey. He arrived at Yarkand and planned to take the Southern Way—the southern portion of the Silk Road—to get back to China.

On his way, Hsuan Tsang passed through the city of Hotan. Going east, the road was very dry and passed into a desert. As Hsuan Tsang described it:

> These sands extend like a drifting flood for a great distance, piled up or scattered according to the wind. There is no trace left behind by travelers, and oftentimes the way is lost, and so they wander hither and thither quite bewildered, without any guide or direction. So travelers pile up the bones of animals as beacons [signals]. There is neither water nor herbage to be found, and hot winds frequently blow. When these winds rise, then both men and beasts become confused and forgetful, and then they remain perfectly disabled. At times sad plaintive notes are heard and piteous cries, so that between the sights and sounds of the desert men get confused and know not whither they go. Hence there are so many who perish in the journey.

When Hsuan Tsang finally did get back to the borders of the China that he knew, he waited to see whether he would be welcomed—or arrested for breaking the travel ban of years earlier. However, the emperor's anger had cooled, and Hsuan Tsang in fact became a kind of local hero, for many people had heard of his brave trip.

A NEW ERA FOR CHINA

The record that Hsuan Tsang kept of his travels is the story of a changing world. Buddhism had been a major religion in Central and East Asia for centuries. Now even in its homeland, India, it was beginning to fade. Soon it would be under heavy attack from both ends of the Silk Road.

Hsuan Tsang also traveled the Silk Road just as China was recovering from several unsettled centuries. Within his lifetime, China had finally united again, under the new T'ang dynasty. This began a golden age for China that would last for three centuries. China was especially able to profit from its strong new dynasty, for Turkish control of Central Asia was collapsing.

Thus, China was now encouraged to spread beyond its Great Wall and to become more expansionist. By the eighth century the Chinese borders had spread north to Lake Balkash and west to the Talas and Jaxartes rivers, where the powerful Ferghana horses still roamed.

During this period Central Asia began to be called Sinkiang, or "New Dominion," meaning the land that was newly dominated by China. (The region of Sinkiang is part of China today.) China's

influence extended even to other lands. Samarkand, (in today's Uzbekistan Soviet Republic) for example, had its own kings, but they could take their thrones only if the Chinese approved of them. The Tibetans, too, bowed to China's power. Earlier they had been under India's influence and had accepted Buddhism as their religion. In the eighth century, their king took a Chinese princess as a bride. China was entering a three-hundred-year period of influence, power, and control.

Buddhist sculptures like these were found throughout Central Asia, from Dunhuang's Cave of the Thousand Buddhas all the way to India. (By Sven Hedin, from his *Through Asia*, 1899)

2

THE SILK ROAD: FROM THE SEVENTH CENTURY TO THE PRESENT

THE T'ANG DYNASTY AND THE OPENING OF CHINA

The T'ang dynasty ruled China from A.D. 618 to 906. Under this dynasty, China expanded its territory a great deal. The country was also somewhat more open to foreigners. During this period the Silk Road was a major lifeline connecting China with the other nations of the world.

The Silk Road was used by jugglers, singers, acrobats, dancers, actors, and magicians, who came to China from Syria, Bactra, and India. Besides these entertainers, the road was used by scholars and monks who wanted to study the ways of the East. At this time China was home to many scholars, including Koreans, Tibetans, and Annamese (from today's country of Vietnam).

Missionaries and religious refugees also found safety in China. Many different religions were welcomed and protected there at this time.

The Zoroastrian Religion. The Zoroastrian religion was founded by Zoroaster, a religious teacher and prophet who lived in Persia in the sixth and fifth centuries B.C. (Zoroaster was the Greek version of the prophet's name; his own people knew him as

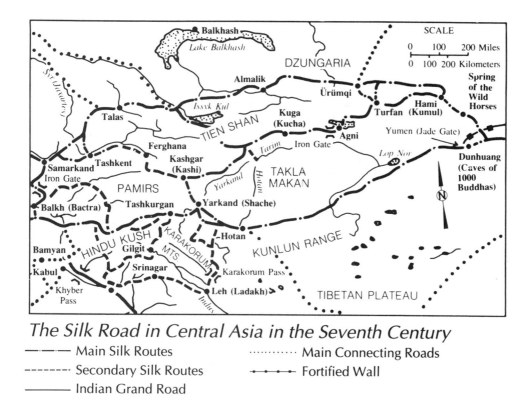

The Silk Road in Central Asia in the Seventh Century

— · — Main Silk Routes   ············ Main Connecting Roads

- - - - - Secondary Silk Routes   ·—·—·— Fortified Wall

———— Indian Grand Road

Zarathustra.) According to this religion, the world is full of good and evil spirits that fight for control. The war between these spirits will eventually lead to the victory of the good.

This religion flourished in Persia until Alexander the Great conquered that land in the fourth century. Then it went into a decline. It was revived again in Persia and made its way to China in the fifth century A.D. There it was protected under the T'ang dynasty.

Nestorian Christianity. Another religion that was protected in China was that of the Nestorians. These were a group of Christians who were regarded as heretical by the major Christian denominations.

Christians believe that their spiritual leader, Jesus Christ, was the son of God as well as being a human being. They believe that both the human and the divine were united in this one being. Nestorians, however, believed that Jesus was two distinct people—one human, one divine.

This belief was begun by Nestorius, who had been the Patriarch, or head, of the Eastern Orthodox Church in Constantinople during the fifth century A.D. At that time there were two major Christian churches, which between them covered much of Europe and the Middle East.

However, Nestorius's belief was not acceptable to either of these churches. His followers fled from Syria to China in the seventh century. They arrived in Chang'an, where a monument commemorating their arrival lasted into modern times. The Chinese emperor himself decreed that the Nestorian Christians should be free to practice and spread their religion. He said:

> The way has more than one name, and wise men have more than one method. Knowledge is such that it may suit all countries, so that all creatures may be saved. The virtuous...[Nestorians] came from afar, bringing books and pictures to our capital...it is right that this teaching should spread freely though the world.

Manichaeism. A third religion —Manichaeism—was welcome in China but practically nowhere else. This faith was founded by Mani, who was probably of Persian origin and who lived during the third century B.C. This way of thinking took elements from Christianity, Zoroastrianism, and an early religion called Gnosticism.

Like Zoroastrians, Manichees also believed that the world was the battleground for good and evil. Manichaeism said that there was an evil spirit who had as much—or almost as much—power as the good one. The Christians also considered Manichaeism heretical, and it survived in the West only until about the sixth century. In the East, however, it lasted until the 13th century.

Trade Continues. It was not only religions that did well in the open climate under the T'ang dynasty. Merchants also carried on much trade, especially along the Silk Road. The western dialects of the merchants mixed with those of Central and East Asia, so that the Chinese language began to reflect the new mix of people and cultures that was coming into the country.

THE RISE OF THE MOSLEMS

The seventh century was a time of great change on the western end of the Silk Road. Eventually these changes would lead once again to the closing of the road and to China pulling back within its borders.

These changes began in a climate of conflict and competition in the Middle East. For centuries, the Byzantine and Persian empires had been in conflict (see Chapter 1).

Persia and Byzantium. At this time, the Middle East was part of an empire called the Byzantine Empire. This empire had been the eastern half of the old Roman Empire and followed the Eastern Orthodox version of Christianity.

The Persian Empire, spreading out of the territory that today is the country of Iran, followed different religions, including Zoroastrianism. The Byzantines greatly resented this empire, for it had insisted on controlling all silk trade that passed through its borders. Because the Silk Road passed from China through Persia, Persia had a virtual monopoly on the Chinese silk to be traded with the West.

Sometimes the Persians even cut off the Silk Road entirely. Then the Byzantines could trade with the East only by sea, on the Spice Route. Over time, this struggle weakened both the Byzantines and the Persians.

The Rise of Islam. With both great empires weak, the stage was set for a new power in the Middle East—the Moslems. Moslems are the followers of a religion called Islam. This religion has been a powerful force in the world since it was first founded in the seventh century A.D. and continues to be a powerful force today.

Islam was founded in Arabia (today's Saudi Arabia) by the prophet Muhammad. This religion grew out of Judaism and Christianity and holds that there is only one supreme God whom all humans must worship. According to Islam, Adam, Noah, Abraham, Moses, and Jesus are all God's prophets, but the last and greatest prophet of all is Muhammad.

Almost as soon as Islam was founded, it spread quickly through the Middle East, North Africa, and even into some parts of Asia. It swept quickly through Persia, suppressing Zoroastrianism. While the territory became almost totally Moslem, some parts of Persia were left semi-independent. Prime among these were Tabiristan, which circled the southern rim of the Caspian Sea (today, part of Iran), and Armenia, between the Caspian and Black seas (today, one of the republics of the Soviet Union).

The Byzantines and the Moslems fought over control of the part of the Silk Road that passed through Persia. But by the middle of the eighth century, the Moslems had swallowed all the former

Persian territories. They had even tried to take over Constantinople—but without success.

The Moslem-Chinese Battle.

It seemed inevitable that the Chinese and the Moslems would clash at some stage—and this was a factor that led to the eventual closing of the Silk Road. Here is how it happened:

The Moslems were moving eastward, helped by their new allies, the Tibetans. In 751 they met the advance guard of the Chinese at the Talas River and engaged in hostilities. Although the Chinese were defeated, the Moslems did not follow them east. Instead, they let the Talas River stand as the dividing line between Moslem and Chinese territory.

One unexpected result of this battle was that a number of skilled Chinese silk-weavers and papermakers were captured and taken to Syria, which by then had become a Moslem country. There they began to produce high-quality silk cloth and paper.

Both Persian and Tabiristan kings turned to the Chinese for help. But it was no use. Both lost their thrones to the Moslems and took refuge in the Chinese city of Chang'an (Xi'an). With the Moslems and Chinese on hostile terms, the part of the Silk Road that ran

A caravan leaves the bustle of daily life in Ankara on a trading journey to distant lands. (Detail from *The Bazaar at Ankara*, by J. V. Van Mour, Rijksmuseum, Amsterdam)

through Persia was closed. Once again China was cut off from part of the world.

New Trade Openings with the Byzantines. However, even though the Silk Road was closed, China continued to trade with other peoples. The peoples of the Byzantine Empire wanted the silk trade to continue. They tried to open up a new northern route across the Eurasian Steppe to China.

But the Eurasian Steppe was too unsettled to be a reliable trade route. Travel there was difficult and dangerous. Besides, Europe— the old silk market for the Byzantines—was now poor and divided. The Byzantines couldn't sell as much silk as before to the Europeans, so they had less need to trade with the Chinese.

The Moslem-Chinese Alliance. Despite the hostilities that had erupted between the Chinese and the Moslems, the Moslems were still eager to trade with China. And they wanted to maintain good relations for other reasons. Within 40 years of the battle of the Talas River, China and the Moslems had allied against the Tibetans, who were still a dangerous presence on the Silk Road.

Silk was no longer the primary trading commodity; the Moslems sought other things of value in the East. The prophet Muhammad himself had once said "Seek for Learning, though it be as far away

Filing across the Iranian plateau, this caravan is headed for the caravanserai (rest stop) on the right. (By Engelbert Kaempfer, c. 1680, MS. Sloane 5232, British Library)

as China." Merchants, scholars, and travelers passed back and forth between Moslem and Chinese territories, exchanging both products and ideas. (Most actual Moslem-Chinese trade, however, took place by sea, on the Spice Route.)

The End of Religious Tolerance. These were sad days for the Buddhist religion throughout the East. When the Moslems came, they destroyed the Buddhist temples. They also destroyed parts of ancient and beautiful cities, such as Balkh (currently part of Afghanistan).

The Chinese, too, had begun to veer away from Buddhism to a new moral and religious system—Confucianism. In A.D. 845 the Confucians outlawed all other religions. Temples were smashed, and Buddhist monks and nuns were attacked. Buddhism, Nestorian Christianity, and most other religions that had found safety in China survived. But they never regained their former strength.

Confucianism. The Confucian philosophy, however, continued to be powerful in China for centuries to come. Confucianism comes from the teachings of Confucius, a Chinese *sage*, or wise man, who lived during the sixth and fifth centuries B.C. In many ways Confucianism continues to affect Chinese teachings and ethics today, even though it is no longer officially practiced.

Confucius was born during a time of tyranny and warfare, and his teachings urged a system of morality and good government, so that there would be peace, stability, and justice in his country. The content of Confucianism changed over the centuries, but essentially, Confucianism always was more a practical guide on how to conduct oneself in the world, rather than a spiritual system that explained the supernatural or the miraculous.

Much of Confucius's teachings concern the Confucian Golden Rule—if you wish to be treated well when you are subordinate to someone else, you must treat well those who are subordinate to you. Society should be managed with *jen* —"human-heartedness"—a kind way of treating others. You could be sure of treating others well was by following certain rituals—ways of acting—and forms of etiquette—politeness.

From the third to the seventh centuries A.D., Confucianism was less popular than Buddhism and another religion, Taoism. Unlike Confucianism, both of these religions are based on faith in unseen and powerful spirits. Under the T 'ang dynasty, however, Confucianism was revived and became an important force in the government. (In later dynasties, other forms of Confucianism appeared, some of which combined elements from Buddhism and Taoism.)

TURKS, MONGOLS, AND JURCHENS

The End of the T'angs. The T'angs had turned to Confucianism to strengthen their government. Eventually, however, they were faced with many revolts and a weakening of their power. More and more often they called on northern peoples to help them restore order. Eventually their government would fall—and the control of the Silk Road would once again fall into the hands of many different peoples.

In 755 the Uighur Turks, from the Turfan region, helped put down a revolt in Chang'an, which was then the Chinese capital. When the T'angs finally fell from power at the beginning of the 10th century, a Turkish regime took over the eastern end of the Silk Road. The capital was moved from Chang'an to a city called Kaifeng.

Eventually a new dynasty called the Sungs ruled all of central and southern China. But northern China was broken apart. For several centuries it passed back and forth between the rules of various northern peoples, and this affected the flow of trade that was carried on along the Silk Road.

The Rule of the Mongols. One northern people who ruled in China were the Mongols. The Mongols had first been summoned to aid the Chinese in the 10th century A.D. when the Chinese needed help in expelling the Turks from the Huang region. The Khitans, a Mongol people from Manchuria north of the Gulf of Bo Hai, came to help—and stayed. In fact, they ruled part of the Silk Road, sharing its eastern end with other non-Chinese people. They set their capital north of the Great Wall and west of the Gulf of Bo Hai, pulling trade northwest as well.

The Turkish form of the Khitan name—Khitai—came to be the name for all of northern China. Khitai is still the Russian word for China, while the European version became "Cathay."

The Sung dynasty in southern China was hostile to the Khitans, but could not win northern China back from them. In fact, the Sung dynasty had to pay large amounts of tribute—protection—to keep the Khitans from continuing a war against them. For centuries afterward it paid the Khitans gold, silk, and other precious goods to keep its northern borders free from raids.

China's Influence Grows. China's influence continued to grow in other ways, despite its depleted power. The peoples who had settled along the eastern half of the Silk Road became more and more "Chinese" in their outlook. They took on Chinese customs, Chinese skills, and also the Buddhist religion.

The Buddhists were doing their best to keep their religion alive. Buddhist monks in Central Asia copied and recopied the sacred texts, so that they would have a better chance of being preserved for the future. In the city of Dunhuang in 1906, a French explorer discovered a huge storehouse of these ancient Buddhist texts. Some of them were translations that had been made by Hsuan Tsang himself (see Chapter 1). The room holding them had been sealed up—probably in some time of danger—in about A.D. 1015.

The Jurchens. In the 12th century, the Sung dynasty repeated the mistake it had made with the Khitans. It invited the Jurchens, a wild nomadic people from Siberia (today the northeastern part of the Soviet Union), to help them drive out the Khitans. The Jurchens not only drove out the Khitans to the north and west, but they also drove out the Sung to the south. China's borders shrank all the way down to the Yangtze River.

In the north, the Jurchen founded the Chin dynasty. Although they were invaders, they quickly adopted Chinese ways. Their empire stretched from Manchuria to the Huang and Wei river valleys. Now there were three eastern empires—the Chin, the Sung, and the Hsi-Hsia, rulers of Tibet—that reached as far south and east as the Jade Gate in the city of Yumen.

ASSASSINS AND CRUSADERS

The final great period of the Silk Road lasted from the invasion of the Seljuk Turks in the 11th century through the end of the Yuan Dynasty in 1368. During the first half of this period, various groups continued to fight for power over China. As before, this had a disruptive effect on China's trade. China continued to form and re-form its borders, to establish and reestablish its relations with the outside world.

However, a new people began to figure prominently in Chinese affairs—the Europeans. Although in the 11th century the Europeans had been woefully ignorant about China, they had gradually gained more knowledge of and interest in this rich land. As they did, they sought to take a piece of the valuable China trade for themselves. Eventually, many centuries later, it would be Europeans who would control China's trade routes and even some parts of China itself.

European Trade. In the 11th century, however, the Europeans had lost the contact with the East that they had enjoyed before the Moslems spread. Some trade goods—though far fewer than in previous times—still reached Europe via Moslem lands. But, like the Persians before them, the Moslems also blocked direct European travel to the East. Instead, Syrians, Jews, and Greeks in western Asia played their old roles as go-betweens. They traded from China to the Moslem countries, and the Moslem countries were the ones to trade with Europe.

Seljuk Turks: The Assassins. A major blow to Silk Road trade came in the 11th century at the hands of the Seljuk Turks. This invading people came down from the Iranian Plateau onto the Mesopotamian plain (in modern-day Iraq). They quickly adopted the Moslem religion and culture of the people whom they had conquered. But in their case, this cultural adoption took a strange twist. When the Turks conquered Persia, they also took Tabiristan, the region where the Silk Road passes just south of the Caspian Sea. There the Seljuk Turks founded a secret sect called the Assassins. This group used murder in order to keep political control. Their technique was so effective that, even today, we call a political murderer an assassin.

The Crusaders. Farther to the west, the Seljuk Turks had taken over much of the Byzantine Empire. Although this territory had already been converted from Christianity to Islam, the previous rulers had allowed Christian pilgrims (religious travelers) to cross the territory on their way to their holy cities in Israel.

The Seljuk Turks changed that policy. They no longer wanted Christians to travel through their lands. This change in policy gave rise to the series of wars known as the Crusades, which were waged by the Europeans against the Turks. Apart from the religious significance of the Crusades, the wars were also fought as a way of gaining control of the trade routes and other economic benefits.

The first Crusade began in 1095 and the last ended in 1291. For a while during that period, the Europeans were partly successful in their goal of taking over the Middle East and making it a Christian area once again. Temporarily, at least, there were several Christian states along the coasts of Syria and Palestine (the modern-day countries of Jordan and Israel).

During the actual fighting, trade on the western end of the Silk Road was disrupted. But for many years during the Crusades the Middle East was relatively peaceful, whether under Christian or Moslem states. During these times goods traveled along the western part of the Silk Road to Antioch. From there goods were ferried to Europe by the ships of the rising Italian city-states, notably Genoa, Venice, and Pisa.

These Italian city-states were to be of crucial importance to the history of China—and the world—in the centuries to come. Their need for eastern goods encouraged them to explore both land and sea routes to the Far East. As they became stronger, they looked for ways to bypass the Moslems and trade directly with China, India, and other Far Eastern lands, seeking spices, jewels, porcelain, and silks. Later, Spain and Portugal would sponsor journeys undertaken by Italian sailors, which led to the discovery of the Americas.

In the 11th and 12th centuries, however, the Europeans were content to restrict their trade to the sea routes between the Middle East and the nations of southern Europe. Their real power in the Far East was not to come for another few centuries.

GENGHIS KHAN AND THE MONGOL PEACE

Early in the 13th century, China was again invaded. However, this invader was to unify and strengthen China. He and his people founded a dynasty that put almost all of the Silk Road in the hands of one power, for the first—and last—time in history.

The young leader was named Temujin. Early in the 13th century, he had united the Mongol peoples on the Eurasian Steppe. Temujin took the name of Genghis Khan and went on to conquer much of Asia. Genghis Khan and his men took control of Balkh (in modern Afghanistan) and then Rayy (near the modern city of Tehran, in Iran). They took Armenia and then Tiflis (currently called Tbilisi, the capital of the Georgian Soviet Republic).

Still during the first wave of his invasion, Genghis Kahn also pushed down through the Hindu Kush mountains into India. There he began his drive toward China. In this first bite, he took the Chinese territory north of the Huang River. His sons quickly drove across the Eurasian Steppe as far as Hungary, in eastern Europe.

Although China was closer to the Mongolian homeland, it took the Mongols longer to conquer it than to win the western parts of Asia. But by 1260, the Mongols had done it. They formed a new dynasty—the Yuan dynasty.

Achievements of the Yuan Dynasty. Under Mongol rule, almost the whole of the Silk Road was in the hands of one power. Other powers still held the Syrian coast. But travelers could enter Mongol territory from the north and then travel all the way to China.

The Mongol Empire was also open to the world. The Mongols welcomed traders, envoys, and even missionaries from abroad. For one short century—1260 through 1368—travelers could move easily in Asia. In fact, they had not one but two land routes: the Silk Road and the more northerly Eurasian Steppe Route (see Chapter 3).

The Mongol headquarters was in Karakorum, out on the Eurasian Steppe. Their Chinese capital was in the northern city of Beijing—the city that is the capital of China today. Both cities were more easily reached by the Eurasian Steppe Route, which was a busier trade route during this period than the Silk Road.

MARCO POLO AND THE EUROPEAN CONNECTION

The Silk Road was the route used by Marco Polo, the famous Italian explorer. Polo left Venice in 1271 and returned there in 1295. He spent the 24 years in between on a long trip to China.

Polo's trip to China was highly significant. It was the first time in modern history that a European had reached the lands of the Far East. The news and trade goods that he brought back to Italy were to play an important role in the European's desire to expand their trade eastward during the next centuries.

Marco Polo's trip was also significant for another reason. Polo's story was written down by his secretary, Rustichello, and the story tells us much about what life was like for travelers and residents in the China of Marco Polo's day.

On the Way to China. Marco Polo entered the Silk Road in Armenia. Many cities in that region produced silk and woven fabrics, as fine as any he had seen anywhere. Remember that 1,000 years earlier, the Byzantine Empire in this region had been starved for silk. Now both silk and good weavers were plentiful.

Polo went on through Persia. On the Iranian Plateau, he found that the local people had built a reputation for breeding horses, which they exported to India. They also bred asses, which they supplied to traders, for carrying goods along the Silk Road. Polo believed these animals to be the finest in the world. They needed to be—the Silk Road was no easy trip.

[These asses] eat little, carrying heavy loads, and travel long distances in a single day, enduring toil beyond the power of horses or mules. For the merchants of these parts, when they travel from one country to another, traverse vast deserts, that is to say dry, barren, sandy regions, producing no grass or fodder suitable for horses, and the wells and sources of fresh water lie so far apart that they must travel by long stages if their beasts are to have anything to drink. Since horses cannot endure this, the merchants use only these asses, because they are swift coursers [runners] and steady amblers [walkers], besides being less costly to keep....They also use camels, which likewise carry heavy loads and are cheap to maintain.

Marco Polo also discovered that the Mongol rule had brought some order to the route, which once had been shared among many warring nations.

Among the people of these kingdoms [of Persia] there are many who are brutal and bloodthirsty. They are forever slaughtering one another; and, were it not for fear of the government...they would do great mischief to traveling merchants. The government imposes severe penalties upon them and has ordered that along all dangerous routes the inhabitants at the request of the merchants shall supply good and efficient escorts from district to district for their safe conduct on payment of two or three groats [type of coin] for each loaded beast according to the length of the journey. Yet, for all that the government can do, these brigands [robbers] are not to be deterred from frequent depredations [robberies]. Unless the merchants are well armed and equipped with bows, they slay and harry them unsparingly.

Inside China. Polo moved across the Iranian Plateau, into the Pamir mountains, and out into Sinkiang. He was struck time and again with the contrasts between the valley oases "where there is rich herbage [grass], fine pasturage, fruit in plenty, and no lack of anything" and the long stretches of desert in which no water or home was to be found.

In Polo's account we also see pictures of once-great cities gone to ruin. Not only were the old Buddhist temples gone—pulled down

during the suppression of Buddhism by the Moslems and Confucians —but Moslem mosques were gone as well.

The great Moslem traveler Ibn Battuta visited the region somewhat farther north 50 years after Polo's journey. He also found the ruins of Moslem mosques. He said that some of the damage had been to punish the Moslems who had revolted against Mongol rule. The rest of the damage was simply the ravages of time. According to Ibn Battuta, Samarkand had once been "one of the greatest and finest cities, and most perfect of them in beauty." But when he was there, he found

> There were formerly great palaces on its bank, and constructions which bear witness to the lofty aspirations of the townsfolk, but most of this is obliterated, and most of the city itself has also fallen into ruins. It has no city wall, and no gates, and there are gardens inside it.

Ibn Battuta left the Silk Road to enter India. But Marco Polo continued on, to give us a picture of the Southern Way (the southern part of the Silk Road—see Chapter 1). This route was then 1,500 years old.

Like so many Asian cities, Samarkand is dotted with ruins that speak of its great past. (By D. Ivanoff, reprinted in H. Yule and H. Cordier, *The Book of Ser Marco Polo,* 1903)

High in the Pamir Mountains. As Polo left Central Asia, he passed into the Pamir mountains, a region of

> many narrow passes and natural fortresses, so that the inhabitants are not afraid of any invader breaking in to molest them. Their cities and towns are built on mountain tops or sites of great natural strength.

Many earlier writers had written that the Pamirs were difficult or dangerous. But Polo had mostly good words to say about them. He raved about the "lush growth," the "copious springs of the purest waters," the choice trout and other fish, and especially the pure mountain air. Perhaps his attitude comes from the fact that he had been sick with a fever when he entered the mountains. That was the place where he became well again, and so he came to love the people and the mountains. He also may have spent more time there than other travelers, so he had time to adjust to the lack of oxygen in the thin mountain air.

Polo's Journey Continues. Polo continued to observe interesting habits and customs on his way. According to him, the Mongols had no one religion at this time. Instead, he said, they honored the holy days of all in order to win favor from all the gods. In Siankiang Polo found Moslems, Nestorian Christians, Buddhists, and people of other religions as well.

Like Silk Road travelers for centuries before him, Polo was worried about crossing the salt flats around the Lop Nor (the dry salt swamp):

> After leaving Charchan [Qargan], the road runs for fully five days through sandy wastes, where the water is bad and bitter, except in a few places...At the end of the five days' journey...is a city which stands on the verge of the Great Desert. It is here that men take in provisions for crossing the desert...

There travelers rested for a week "to refresh themselves and their beasts." The rest was needed because they had to travel "for a day and a night" between water holes. Even then, the water was often "bitter and brackish [half salty]," and enough only for small parties of 50 to a 100 people and their animals.

Polo also had to face the old fears—real and imaginary—that were always brought on by the towering, shifting sand dunes of the Takla Makan Desert:

From the earliest times to today, travelers in the Takla Makan Desert felt wariness and sometimes downright fear when passing along its towering sand dunes. (By Sven Hedin, from his *Through Asia*, 1899)

When a man is riding by night through this desert and something happens to make him loiter and lose touch with his companions, by dropping asleep or for some other reason, and afterwards he wants to rejoin them, then he hears spirits talking in such a way that they seem to be his companions. Sometimes, indeed, they even hail him by name. Often these voices make him stray from the path, so that he never finds it again. And in this way many travelers have been lost and have perished. And sometimes in the night they are conscious of a noise like the clatter of a great cavalcade of riders away from the road; and, believing that these are some of their own company, they go where they hear the noise and, when day breaks, find they are victims of an illusion and in an awkward plight. And there are some who, in crossing this desert, have seen a host of men coming towards them and, suspecting that they were robbers, have taken flight; so, having left the beaten track and not knowing how to return to it, they have gone helplessly astray. Yes, and even by daylight men hear these spirit voices, and often you fancy you are listening to the strains of many instruments, especially drums, and the clash of arms. [Scientists today believe that these noises may come from swirling winds and avalanches of sand around the towering sand dunes.] For this reason bands of travelers make a point of keeping very close together. Before they go to sleep they set up a sign pointing in the direction in which they have to travel. And round the necks of all their beasts they fasten little bells, so that by listening to the sound they may prevent them from straying off the path.

Polo Goes North. So far Polo had followed the old main route of the Silk Road. But now he went off to the north. He did not even mention the once-great cities of Dunhuang, Chang'an, Luoyang, and Kaifeng. By this we see how much the center of China had shifted northward, toward Beijing. This change had come with the Mongols, who had pushed China's center closer to their own northern homeland.

Marco Polo's Journey and China's Future. In 1295, when Marco Polo returned to Venice, the Europeans were not prepared to set up their own trade with China. They were still willing to depend on Syrian, Greek, and Jewish merchants to bring goods west to the Middle East, where Italian ships could then pick them up. Two centuries later, however, in 1492, the Spaniards would sponsor another Italian explorer, Christopher Columbus, to find a new sea route to the East. Columbus never reached India or China—but his discovery of North and South America was motivated by the same desire that had sparked Marco Polo's journey. Polo's reports on the riches of the East were to help fuel first European exploration, then European conquering of eastern lands.

THE END OF THE SILK ROAD

Last Days of the Mongols. The Mongols made many important changes on the Silk Road and in China as a whole. They chose

Beijing as their winter capital and called it Khanbaligh—city of the Khan, or ruler. The Chinese name, Beijing, meant "northern capital." The Mongols' summer capital was out on the Mongolian plateau. The Mongols called it Shang-tu. Europeans called it Xanadu.

Neither the winter or the summer capital was located near the old eastern end of the Silk Road. Instead, travelers focused on this new northern center. Under the Mongols, the Silk Road remained a somewhat important trade route. But when the Mongol's Yuan dynasty fell in 1368, the days of the Silk Road came to an end.

The Ming Dynasty. After the Yuan came the Ming. Under this dynasty, China closed its borders more tightly than ever before. Foreigners were driven from the land. The Great Wall was rebuilt, this time with sturdy stone walls that can be seen even today. These developments sent trade on the Silk Road into a final decline.

Beyond the Great Wall. On the other side of China's Great Wall, Islam spread, reaching even the Mongols. By the 15th century the Mongols had adopted Islam. When the Turks conquered the Central Asian lands that the Mongols held, the Turks, too, maintained Islam as the dominant religion. Gone were most traces of the once-great Buddhist culture of Central Asia.

In China, the Ch'ing dynasty of the Manchus replaced the Ming dynasty in the 17th century. This dynasty was to remain in power until the Chinese revolution of 1912, when the dynastic system was abolished and a republic was established under Sun Yat-sen.

Under the Ch'ing in the 17th century, China did expand westward into Central Asia once more. But the old Silk Road never revived. This was because the Silk Road had been oriented toward communication with the Mediterranean and the European nations of Italy and Greece. By the 17th century, however, European power was centered in northern Europe, in such countries as France, the Netherlands, and England. The northern Europeans were the new market, and Chinese trade routes were affected accordingly.

Central Asia and the Europeans. By the 19th century Central Asia was in the hands of mostly Mongolian or Turkish peoples in a number of small states. China had once held many of these lands but had lost control over them. The Europeans now saw them as easy conquests for themselves. The Russians moved down from the Eurasian Steppe into the region that is now the Soviet Republic of Turkestan. The British crossed the Karakorum Mountains to penetrate the desert heartland of Asia. French and Swedish explorers also followed this route.

It was at this time that Europeans named China's old trade route "the Silk Road." Explorers found traces of Central Asia's old kingdoms. The European's interest in Asia was economic as well. During the 19th century merchants from England, France, Germany, other European nations as well as the United States were all competing for the "China market." Trade with China was important to all of these nations.

The Chinese often resented the people whom they called "foreign devils." They believed that they were being taken advantage of and that foreign cultures were corrupting the Chinese people. However, the Europeans and the United States were stronger than the Chinese, and they had the military power to force the Chinese to trade.

Trade now no longer took place along the Silk Road. Instead, sea trade took over, especially around the port city of Shanghai.

MODERN TIMES

With the great days of the Silk Road long past, the bazaar in early 20th-century Yarkand was more shabby than exotic. (Royal Geographic Society)

Relations between China and Europe remained stormy for many years. The two greatest turning points in Chinese history were the revolution of 1912, which got rid of the old dynasties and replaced

them with a republic, and the revolution of 1949, which installed a Communist government in China. Both revolutions greatly affected relations with the West.

During the 20th century China expanded its borders one last time. It absorbed the regions of Sianking, Manchuria, Inner Mongolia, and Tibet. The political map of Asia in general changed several times. The great Silk Road cities of Tashkent, Samarkand, Bukhara, and Merv as well as the Caucus region around the Caspian Sea had all become part of the Central Asian or Caucusus republics of the Soviet Union. Afghanistan and Iran were formed as new, modern nations; in both countries the form of government has undergone many changes.

Because of the changing political alliances, it is no longer possible to take the old Silk Road across Asia. However, China and the

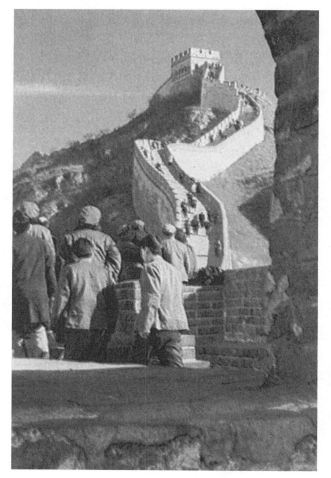

Operating for centuries to keep invaders out and Chinese in, the Great Wall has now become a tourist attraction in itself. (Willie K. Friar, Panama Canal Commission)

country of Pakistan, which borders China, India, and Afghanistan, have made an alliance to build a new route, the Karakorum Highway. This road snakes across the mountains of Kashmir, through passes as high as 19,000 feet, from the Chinese city of Kashgar all the way to Pakistan.

Even today travelers still need their wits about them to travel these routes. Avalanches are a routine occurrence on the Karakorum Highway. They can wipe away a motor convoy as easily as they once destroyed a camel caravan. And whether riding a camel or a Land Rover, a traveler is wise to beware the dangerous mirages of the desert of Takla Makan.

SUGGESTIONS FOR FURTHER READING

Ibn Battuta. *Travels, A.D. 1325–1354*, in 3 volumes (Cambridge: University Press, 1958–71). Hakluyt Society Publications, 2nd series. Translated by H. A. R. Gibb. A fine edition, with helpful maps.

Blunt, Wilfrid. *The Golden Road to Samarkand* (New York: Viking, 1973). A well-illustrated work focusing on famous personages on the Silk Road, from Alexander to Marc Aurel Stein.

Boulnois, L. *The Silk Road* (London: George Allen & Unwin, 1966). Translated from the French by Dennis Chamberlin. A helpful review of the route in classical and early medieval times.

Cable, Mildred, and Francesca French. *Through the Jade Gate and Central Asia: An Account of Journeys in Kansu, Turkestan, and the Gobi Desert* (Boston: Houghton Mifflin, 1927). Travels by missionaries in China.

de Gaury, Gerald, and H. V. F. Winstone, eds. *The Road to Kabul: An Anthology* (London: Quartet Books, 1981). Excerpts of works by modern travelers in Central Asia.

Edwardes, Michael. *East-West Passage: The Travel of Ideas, Arts, and Inventions between Asia and the Western World* (New York: Taplinger, 1971). An interesting review of cross-connections, weighted somewhat toward the modern period.

Franck, Irene M., and David M. Brownstone. *The Silk Road: A History* (New York: Facts On File, 1986). A full, illustrated history from the earliest times to today.

Grousset, René. *The Empires of the Steppes: A History of Central Asia* (New Brunswick, N.J.: Rutgers University Press, 1970). Translated from the French by Naomi Walford. A detailed, classic political history.

————. *In the Footsteps of the Buddha* (New York: Grossman, 1971). Translated from the French by J. A. Underwood. Outlines the spread of Buddhism and the role of the great pilgrims of the East.

Hambly, Gavin, et al. *Central Asia* (London: Weidenfeld & Nicolson, 1969). Volume 16 of the publisher's Universal History. A political history by many writers, stressing modern times.

Hedin, Sven. *The Silk Road* (New York: Dutton, 1938). An account of his retracing of the route.

Herrman, Albert. *An Historical Atlas of China, New Edition* (Edinburgh: Edinburgh University Press, 1966). An extremely useful, detailed work.

Hirth, F. *China and the Roman Orient: Researches into the Ancient and Medieval Relations as Represented in Old Chinese Records* (New York: Paragon, 1966). Reprint of the 1885 Shanghai edition. Reprints and translates some basic texts, stressing identification of references to Western places and artifacts.

Hopkirk, Peter. *Foreign Devils on the Silk Road: The Search for the Lost Cities and Treasures of Chinese Central Asia* (London: John Murray, 1980). Focuses on the modern rediscoverers.

Hudson, G. F. *Europe and China: A Survey of Their Relations from the Earliest Times to 1800* (Boston: Beacon Press, 1961). Reprint of the 1931 edition. A very valuable overview.

Journey Into China (Washington, D.C.: National Geographic Society, 1982). An unusually well-illustrated popular work, with sections on the Silk Road and the Great Wall.

Lattimore, Owen, and Eleanor Lattimore, eds. *Silks, Spices and Empire: Asia Seen Through the Eyes of Its Discoverers* (New York: Delacorte Press, 1968). Part of the Great Explorers series. Selections of firsthand accounts from classical to modern times, with useful editorial overview and comments.

Legg, Stuart. *The Heartland* (New York: Capricorn, 1971). A useful history primarily of the modern period.

Miller, J. Innes. *The Spice Trade of the Roman Empire, 29 B.C.–A.D. 641* (Oxford: Clarendon Press, 1969). Has a scope far wider than the title might indicate, including sections on the trade routes and the carriers.

Mirsky, Jeanette, ed. *The Great Chinese Travelers* (New York: Pantheon, 1964). Well-edited firsthand accounts, longer but fewer in number than in the Lattimore work.

Needham, Joseph. *Science and Civilization in China* (Cambridge: University Press, 1965). Volume 1 of this major work contains a useful historical overview of China's contacts with the West.

Polo, Marco. *The Travels* (Harmondsworth, Middlesex: Penguin, 1958). Translated by Ronald Latham. A readable translation of the classic work, with helpful introduction, notes, and index.

Rostovtzeff, M. *Caravan Cities* (Oxford: Clarendon Press, 1932). Includes a historical survey of the caravan trade, focusing on Mesopotamia.

Schreiber, Hermann. *The History of Roads: From Amber Route to Motorway* (London: Barrie and Rockliff, 1961). Translated from the German by Stewart Thomson. Includes two chapters on the Central Asian caravan routes.

Severin, Timothy. *The Oriental Adventure: Explorers of the East* (Boston: Little, Brown, 1976). Focuses on European travelers in the East, from Marco Polo on.

Stein, Sir Aurel. *On Ancient Central-Asian Tracks: Brief Narrative of Three Expeditions in Innermost Asia and Northwestern China* (New York: Pantheon, 1965). Edited by Jeannette Mirsky. A popular account of his journeys and discoveries.

Teggart, Frederick J. *Rome and China: A Study of Correlations in Historical Events* (Berkeley, Calif.: University of California Press, 1939). A unique work, comparing the effects on each of events in Central Asia, focusing on the period 58 B.C. to A.D. 107.

3

THE AMBASSADOR'S ROAD AND THE BURMA ROAD

THE THREE CENTERS OF CHINA

In its early history China was a small territory far north of today's country of China. Over the years the nation has expanded and shrunk, changing its borders and its rulers on many occasions. Sometimes China was a mighty empire; sometimes it was a small, weak nation.

The oldest part of China is farthest north: a strip of land made up of the valleys of the Wei and Huang (Yellow) rivers. These two valleys both have rich farmland. People have lived and farmed here for thousands of years. One obstacle they have often faced are the Huang's disastrous floods. This river has also sometimes actually changed its course by hundreds of miles.

When the early people of China began to spread out from the north, they moved into the valley of the Yangtze River. (The Yangtze River had two other names: Chang for the eastern half and Jinsha for the western half.) This rich area has long been the economic center of China.

The Chinese eventually moved farther south to the humid southern coast that borders on the China Sea. This area is damp and swampy, the home of many mosquitoes that carry malaria and other serious diseases. For many centuries travelers feared the fevers of this area. A folk poem from the seventh century tells of the fever-

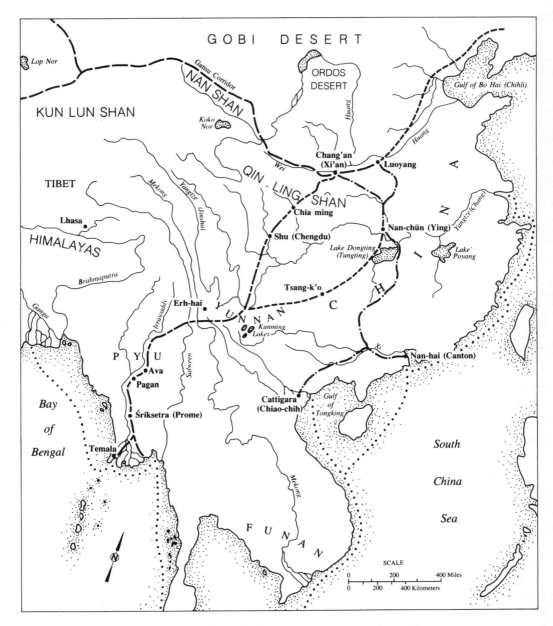

The Ambassador's Road and the Burma Road in the Early Middle Ages

—·—·— Ambassador's Road   -------- Main Connecting Routes

-----— Burma Road   · · · · · · · Spice Route

——— Silk Road

ridden route that led along the coast into Annam (now the country of Vietnam):

> The customs barrier at Ghost Gate—
> Ten men go out,
> Nine men return.

Despite its inhospitable climate and terrain, this region was important to China. Its ports faced the southern seas and were the gateways for sailors and traders from the Middle East and, later, from Europe. Eventually these ports became part of the famous Spice Route. The Spice Route was a network of sea-lanes that sailors and traders used to ship spices, silks, gold, and jewels from China and India back through Arabia and into Europe.

Chinese Roads. Over the centuries these three regions became bound together as part of one great Chinese nation. Expanding from their northern center, these Chinese people spread southward, conquering these other regions and then binding them into one empire by means of roads.

Two of China's most important roads were the Ambassador's Road and the Burma Road. These roads helped unite the many regions of the East into one nation called China. They also helped connect China with the rest of the world during those times when the nation was inclined to reach out or welcome foreigners in. However, the Ambassador's Road got its name from a time when China was *not* receptive to foreigners. At that time, China did not welcome foreign traders or travelers and would accept only a few high-level political ambassadors. Thus, the road came to be known as the Ambassador's Road. (The Burma Road got its name because it connected China to the Southeast Asian region that today includes the country of Myanmar, formerly known as Burma.)

THE AMBASSADOR'S ROAD

The Ambassador's Road was China's great southern route. It began as two roads from two of China's earliest cities. One road came from Chang'an (near the modern city of Xi'an) on the Wei River, and the other started in Luoyang (Loyang) on the Huang River. Both routes joined together to form the Ambassador's Road.

In northern China the staple food is wheat; in southern China it is rice. The Ambassador's Road crosses over the hills that divide the northern wheatlands from the southern wet ricelands, going toward the Yangtze River and following that river's north bank. The road crosses the river after the head of Lake Dongting (Tungting), then goes south to the seaport of Nan-hai. This city later became known to the Europeans as Canton; the Chinese changed its name to Guangzhou or Kwangchow.

A branch road from the Ambassador route also followed the course of the Xi (West) River around the Gulf of Tonkin to the early port of Chiaochih (today's cities of Hanoi and Haiphong) in Annam.

THE BURMA ROAD

The Ambassador's Road was easy to travel, but the Burma Road was more difficult. This road headed into the mountains of southwestern China and then crossed through thick jungles to inner Burma. The Burma Road began in Chang'an and then wended its way south through the steep passes of the Qin Ling (Ch'in-Ling) Mountains. Some of these passes were close to 6,000 feet high.

The road crossed the Yangtze, Mekong, and Salween rivers, to connect with the Irrawaddy River in Burma. Then the road followed the Irrawaddy's east bank down to the Bay of Bengal.

Sometimes an overland road connected the middle of the Irrawaddy with India's Ganges River and great Grand Road. Both the land connection with India and the sea connection with the Bay of Bengal were important Spice Route links, making it possible for China to trade with India and for India to trade with the West.

THE EARLY CHANGES

Before the country of China existed, an early people, the ancestor's of today's Chinese, lived in the Huang River plain. These early Chinese were a Mongol people, related to other Asian peoples. At this time—thousands of years ago—many peoples throughout the world subsisted as nomads. They did not live permanently in one place but traveled throughout huge regions, often with herds of sheep, camels, or goats, constantly looking for new grazing land.

The early Chinese gradually split off from their nomadic kin to the north and west and became a farming people. For these early Chinese farmers, the Huang River plain was a very attractive homeland, for it was rich farmland watered by a powerful river.

By 5,000 years ago, perhaps even earlier, the Chinese had developed a strong, stable farming culture. According to tradition, this was the time that the Chinese also learned how to make silk.

By about 1500 B.C., these early Chinese were using cowrie shells as money, so we know that they had developed a more complicated economy by that point. But these shells didn't come from the Huang River—they came from south of the Yangtze River, which was farther away. Thus, we can deduce that by this time there probably were long trading chains, where goods were exchanged from tribe to tribe over long distances, working their way between north and south. One commodity that was probably traded even at this point in history was silk.

The Early Chinese Expand. From their center on the lower curve of the Huang River, the Chinese spread out into much of what is now northern China. At this time the Burma Road and the Ambassador's Road were no more than tracks in the dirt. But the early Chinese used these tracks to mark the best routes for travel. Traders used both these roads and the rivers to carry goods. Many different kinds of products were traded in those days. From the mountains of today's Shaanxi (Shensi) and Sichuan (Szechuan) provinces came wild animals and precious metals. The Yangtze River basin yielded hides, metals, feathers, bamboo, ivory, pearls, cinnabar (a reddish ore), and tortoise-shells, which were used for religious purposes.

The Yangtze region also sent silk. Silk became so valued and so widely produced that for a while, bolts of silk became the main form of money. Later even taxes had to be paid in silk. The women in each family—including the emperor's family—spent much of the year raising silkworms, which spin the thread that produces silk, and then weaving silk out of the silkworms' thread.

The Chou Dynasty. By 1000 B.C. China was a small nation living under the Chou dynasty. The Chous ruled from 1027 B.C. to 256 B.C. During this period laws were written for the first time, and a new metal, iron, came to be used to make tools. Farmers had also discovered that they could use oxen to help them plow their fields and had invented the ox-drawn plow.

Under the Chou dynasty China expanded into many small states. They all shared a common Chinese language and culture, even though they each had their own rulers. A good road system now

Human carriers were used as "beasts of burden," especially in mountain regions, for centuries—even into the 20th century. (Museum of the American China Trade, Milton, Mass.)

became necessary so that people could travel back and forth between the different states.

Each state had its own system of footpaths and roads. On these traveled messengers bearing word from the far boundaries of the provinces. These roads were well built and maintained, as we can see from this ninth-century B.C. poem:

> The roads of Chou are [smooth] as a whetstone
> Straight as an arrow;
> Ways where the lords and officials pass,
> Ways where the common people look on.

HUANG TI: THE YELLOW EMPEROR

Strong Central Government. In 221 B.C. the Chinese came under a new dynasty—the Ch'in. The Ch'in took control of the whole country and, for the first time, unified all the separate provinces into a single country. Huang Ti, who became known as "the Yellow Emperor," quickly set up a strong central government.

In order to do so, Huang Ti had to take power away from the nobles—the lords who ruled each tiny province. He also had to expand the provincial road system into one single system, centered on the capital of Chang'an. Under Huang Ti a new rule was made: all chariot wheels had to be six feet apart. That way, builders always knew how wide to make their roads.

China Expands. Over the centuries China had expanded to the northwest and east. But expansion east could go only as far as the sea, and expansion to the northwest was blocked by the nomadic people who still lived in Central Asia, especially the Hsiung-nu (known in Europe as the Huns). Therefore, China found expansion easiest to the south and the southwest.

The Chinese rule spread east and covered much of the China coast, from the Yangtze River to Nan-hai. But it went much farther west, out into what today is Szechuan province. Fifty years after Huang Ti's rule, a Chinese writer praised him for the work he did in uniting this new empire:

> He also ordered the building of the post-roads [roads that messengers or "postmen" used to carry messages] all over the empire...around the lakes and rivers, and along the coasts of the sea; so that all was made accessible. These highways were fifty paces wide [probably fifty

feet wide], and a tree was planted every 30 feet along them. The road was made very thick and firm at the edge, and tamped with metal rammers. The planting of the green pine trees was what gave beauty to the roads.

Difficult Engineering. The time of the Ch'in was the period during which the backbone of the Ambassador's Road was set. The

Trestle roads like this one have been built in the Qin Ling Shan (mountains) for thousands of years. (Anonymous photograph)

Ch'in also built a remarkable new road to the southwest, to replace the old, poor paths to Sichuan. However, they faced a difficult engineering job, for this was rocky, mountainous country that did not welcome roads.

Surveyors were sent into the Qin Ling Mountains, whose snow-capped peaks towered over the Wei river valley. There they planned a road that would cross deep river gorges and slide along the sheer rock faces of the mountains. The Chinese engineers proved equal to the task. They built wooden bridges across the deep gorges and hung wooden balconies on the cliff faces. Sometimes they built straight out from narrow ledges. Sometimes they hung balconies from brackets driven right into solid rock.

This new road was a great achievement. The Chinese were so proud of it that they named one part of this road the Linked Cloud Route, to show that this road went so high into the mountains that it allowed travelers to walk from cloud to cloud.

Although the Ch'in are known for their great achievements in both unifying China politically and in building a centralized road system, they were actually in power only for about 25 years. Soon they gave way to a new dynasty, the Han.

THE HAN EMPERORS

The Road System Expands. The Han dynasty lasted for over four centuries and continued to expand on the work that the Ch'in had done, especially on the road system. The Han often used forced labor for the difficult work of building roads—people who were in jail or who had been forced to work for other reasons. However, the Chinese government was directly responsible for building and maintaining roads, and the officials in charge of roads were government officials. Here is a second century B.C. job description for the director of communications:

> [He was to study maps] in order to obtain a perfect knowledge of the mountains, forests, lakes, rivers, and marshes, and to understand the [natural] routes of communication...[He was also responsible for] planting trees and hedges along [the roads]...

In addition, the director had to place guardposts at key points along the road, to make sure that travelers were protected from robbers and bandits who might want to steal their trade goods.

Different Types of Roads. The Chinese roads at this time ranged from simple footpaths to multilane highways. Within the capital and a few other main cities, the main roads were built to carry nine chariots, or even more, side by side. Ring roads around the cities, on the other hand, were only seven chariots wide.

The imperial highways, which linked one city to another, were usually five lanes across. The middle lanes of these highways were supposed to be reserved for the private use of the imperial family and their deputies. In reality, these lanes were seldom reserved, especially far away from the imperial capital. However, Chinese records show that at least one person was executed for the crime of riding in the emperor's lane.

WEST INTO ASIA: THE EXPLORATION OF CHANG CH'IEN

Learning About India. China's road-building skills helped the Han expand farther west into Asia. Before they could expand, however, they had to explore. In 128 B.C. the Han sent a man called Chang Ch'ien to cross Central Asia. This was China's first known mission to the West.

For centuries the Chinese kept the secret of silk manufacturing; here silk workers are feeding silkworms and sorting the cocoons, spun by the worm of silken threads. (From G. Waldo Browne, *The New America and the Far East,* 1901)

Halfway across Asia, at the city of Bactra (now in northern Afghanistan), Chang Ch'ien discovered something surprising: south China bamboo and cloth from Shu were being sold there. When he asked how vendors had gotten hold of these Chinese products, he was told, "Our merchants go to buy them in the markets of Shen-Tu."

This was the first time a Chinese envoy had heard about the great land of Shen-Tu—the Bactrian name for India. It was also the first time that Chang Ch'ien learned of a southern connection between the Yangtze River and the countries below it. Chang Ch'ien immediately saw the advantage of a route from Sichuan to Shen-tu. He went back to the emperor and asked to lead a mission to the southwest, so that he could establish relations with India.

The Way South. Chang Ch'ien did not progress very far on his expedition to India. But he did meet many tribes. He reported that some of them "have no chiefs and were given to robbery; the Chinese envoys would have been killed or captured." He also learned of an elephant-riding state called Tien (Yunnan, or Burma), where Shu traders sometimes went with their goods on unofficial trading missions.

Soon the Hans were slowly pushing west into Burma. As the Chinese expanded, they continued to build more roads. They built a route that crossed the Yangtze near the modern city of Chongqing and then continued southwest past the Kunming Lakes to a point between the upper Mekong and Salween rivers. However, this road was no multilane highway. Some parts were only a few feet wide. The Chinese name for it was The Five Foot Way.

SOUTH INTO ASIA: THE SPICE ROUTE

The Chinese continued to push into Southeast Asia. Later in Han times, their power spread around the coast of Annam. There they took a second major port on the South China Sea—Chiaoh-chih (the modern cities of Hanoi and Haiphong). A main spur of the Ambassador's Road to Nan-hai split off to connect with Chiaoh-chih.

Early Days on the Spice Route. These were some of the great early days on the Spice Route. Sailors from India and Malaya had developed the sea-lanes that linked East to West, carrying spices, gold, jewels, silk, and other eastern products from Asia to the Middle

East. From the Middle East, traders took the goods to Europe, where they were highly prized. Chiaoh-chih and Nan-hai became important ports, for they were the links between China and the Spice Route. The Ambassador's Road, which brought goods overland to these ports, thus also became important.

Traders and Travelers. Trade with the West was conducted by Indians and Malayans. But it also brought other people from farther away to China's shores. In A.D. 120 a group of Syrian jugglers and acrobats arrived in China, perhaps coming through Burma. They were taken north to provide the emperor with his New Year's entertainment. The Chinese chronicle *Hou Han Shu* reported that they could

> conjure, spit fire, bind and release their limbs without assistance, interchange the heads of cows and horses, and dance cleverly with up to a thousand balls.

Magicians and conjurers from India also found their way along the Ambassador's Road to the imperial court.

The Chinese have records of the appearance in A.D. 166 of a mission from "the king of Ta-Ch'in, An-Tun." This may have been a reference to the emperor Aurelius Antoninus of the Roman Empire. Perhaps these were not official Roman envoys but rather merchants trying to open new markets.

When these traders arrived in Annam, they offered ivory, rhinoceros horns, and tortoiseshells to the Chinese. Clearly these were items they had picked up in trading along the way. The *Hou Han Shu* did note, though, that "From that time dates the [direct] intercourse with [the Roman Empire]."

Most travelers on the Ambassador's Road and Burma Road were Chinese, not foreigners. At this time the power base of China was still in the north, with small control over the south. The emperor had set up military-farming colonies in the south, but these were mostly along the main highways. Most people in the south had barely heard of "China."

A TIME OF DECLINE

The Han dynasty ended in A.D. 220, and with it ended a period of strong unity. When the Han dynasty ended, China once again broke up into many smaller states.

For the Ambassador's Road and the Burma Road, this meant the beginning of a long decline. The roads were so badly maintained that carriages could not roll smoothly on them, so travelers used horses instead or else slow, heavy carts that could handle the bumpy track. Rich travelers were carried by others. Many people simply walked.

Carried by porters rather than riding in a wheeled vehicle, this man is protected from the many bumps and holes in the road. (By Thomas Allom, from G. N. Wright, *China in a Series of Views*, 1843)

CHINA REUNITED

The T'ang Dynasty. When the T'ang dynasty came to power in A.D. 618, the process of reunification of the Chinese provinces began. Like the Han centuries before, the T'ang sent military forces into the south to form colonies and rule the native peoples. They took over the peoples of the south China coast. Even today these peoples still call themselves T'ang Jen—People of T'ang—while their central Chinese neighbors call themselves Han Jen—people of Han.

There were good reasons why the T'ang wanted control over Nan-hai and the rest of the south coast. Followers of Islam were

In rough country and elsewhere, much traffic proceeded on foot, like the small party heading away from the settlement into the mountains. (From G. Waldo Browne, *The New America and the Far East*, 1901)

quickly spreading their Moslem religion through the part of western Asia known as the Middle East. Arab sailors from the powerful new Moslem kingdoms were becoming active on the Spice Route and were joining the Indians and Malays in Nan-hai. Thus, it was vital that the Chinese maintain control of this strategic city.

Trade and the Ambassador's Road. With all this increased trade on the Spice Route, the Ambassador's Road became more important, because Chinese goods traveled along it to the Spice Route seaports. In the eighth century minister Chang Chiu-ling was assigned to repair and rebuild the southern part of the Ambassador's Road. He wrote a poem to describe the old road:

> Formerly, an abandoned road in the east of the pass,
> An unswerving course: you clambered [climbed] aloft
> On the outskirts of several miles of heavy forest,
> With flying bridges, clinging to the brink
> Halfway up a thousand fathoms of layered cliffs...

Chang Chiu-ling also wrote about the reasons to repair the road:

The several nations from beyond the sea
Use it daily for commercial intercourse;
Opulence of teeth, hides, feathers, furs;
Profits in fish, salt, clams, cockles.

Silk was also a profitable trade good. All these things and more brought foreigners to Nan-hai, including Indians, Malayans, Indochinese (those from the southeast Asian peninsula), Persians, and Arabs. These foreigners formed an international merchant class within the old port city.

Relations with Foreigners. Relations between foreigners and the Chinese were not always smooth. Chinese officials, many of whom were corrupt, tightly controlled foreign merchants. Sometimes the situation was so bad that Western merchants left Nan-hai and went to Chiaoh-chih, where they were treated better. Sometimes foreign merchants took matters into their own hands: in the middle of the eighth century, a group of Arabs and Persians raided Nan-hai, looting and burning the city. For several decades after that, Chiaoh-chih was the main Chinese port.

There were also revolts in Nan-hai, because it was located on the wild frontiers of China and many local rulers wanted more independence from the central Chinese government. The most serious revolt took place in the middle of the ninth century. According to Chinese records, 120,000 foreign merchants were massacred. This revolt had serious consequences for the city itself, because during it the great mulberry groves that fed the precious silkworms were destroyed. Nan-hai was ruined, and importance returned to Chiaoh-chih. Nan-hai did not fully recover until modern times.

Despite the troubles in Nan-hai, during these T'ang times China became more accessible to foreigners. Foreigners in large numbers traveled along the roads, and some settled in China, although they were closely watched if they did so.

Trouble in Burma. During this period the Burma Road was used far less than the Ambassador's Road. However, in A.D. 698 the governor of Sichuan province faced trouble from the Burmese people. In order to avoid confrontation, the Chinese pulled back to the north and closed the southern part of the Burma Road. This part stayed closed for centuries; the northern part, however, between Chang'an and Shu, stayed in regular use.

At Beijing China's great waterway, the Grand Canal, met the camel trains from across the Eurasian Steppe. (Museum of the American China Trade, Milton, Mass.)

The End of the T'ang. The T'ang dynasty fell in the 10th century. When it fell, China became far weaker and less united and was under constant attack from the nomadic peoples in the north. Under the new dynasty—the Sung—the Chinese moved their capital south, first to Kaifeng, then to Hangzhou (Hangchow).

During this time, the Ambassador's Road lost some of its significance. Most roads were neglected, and canals became the preferred means of travel. Over the centuries the Chinese had built many canals to connect their rivers, so that boats could carry goods from one end of the country to the other. Grain, salt, and other bulk products were sent this way.

Often water buffaloes were used to pull the boats or barges along the canal. Japanese travelers in the ninth century once saw over three dozen salt barges, two or three abreast, being pulled along one side canal by just two water buffaloes. On the main canal, the salt barges might be three to five abreast, stretching for miles.

When the Sung dynasty was forced south, much of China's cultural center moved with it. By the 12th century the southern territories had become fully part of China for the first time in history.

THE MONGOL CONQUEST

In 1260 a nomadic Central Asian people called the Mongols came out of inner Asia and conquered China. Their dynasty, the Yuan, helped to change China in many lasting ways as they rebuilt, restored, and expanded Chinese structures and institutions.

Moving North. The Mongols built their capital in the north and called it Khanbaligh. Their great city awed everyone who saw it, including Europeans used to the splendors of Venice and Rome. Except for short periods, Khanbaligh has remained China's capital ever since. It has had many different names, including its current name of Beijing, or "Northern Capital."

Marco Polo Visits China. One way that we know about life in China under the Yuan is from the records of Marco Polo, an Italian explorer who traveled to China. He arrived in Beijing in 1275, only 15 years after the Mongols took control of China, but he reported that the main roads of the land were all linked with the new capital and that they had all been restored and revived:

> Now you must know the Great Khan has bidden that on the highroads along which his messengers, as well as merchants and other people travel, trees should be planted on both sides, at a distance of two paces from one another. And truly, they are so high and big, that they can be seen from afar. The Great Khan has had this done so that people should be able to see the roads and not miss their way, for you will find these trees even along desert roads; and then they are of great comfort to traders and wayfarers...on rocky mountains, where it [planting trees] would be impossible, he has stone cairns [piles of stones heaped up high] and pillars set up to show the way. And he has certain barons to whom he has committed the task of seeing to it that those roads are constantly kept in good condition.

Because trees could not have grown so much in only 15 years, Polo was obviously seeing the work of an earlier dynasty, but he also perceived the importance that the Mongols gave to roads.

The Mongols' vast empire stretched from one end of Asia to the other. Under their rule, for the first and last time it was possible to cross the entire continent and remain under the power of a single ruler. To govern this huge territory, they needed a good road communication system. Marco Polo praised that system:

> the way the Great Khan's messenger-service works is truly admirable; it is indeed arranged in a most excellent manner....the envoy of the Great Khan who leaves...[Beijing] and rides twenty-five miles, reaches at the end of that stage...a horse-post station. There the envoy finds a very large and fine palace, where the great Khan's envoy lodge, with splendid beds, furnished with rich silk sheets, and with everything else that an important envoy may need. And if a king should go there, he should be splendidly lodged. Here the envoys also find no less than four hundred horses, always kept there by the Great

Khan's orders, in readiness for any envoys of his that he may send somewhere.

And even when the envoys have to traverse [cross]...mountainous regions, without horses or hostels, the Great Khan has had post-stations built there, with...all the other things, such as horses and harness, that the other stations have. Only the distances are larger, for they are placed at thirty-five, and even more than forty miles, from one another. The Great Khan also sends people to live there and till the soil, performing the necessary services for the posts. Thus large villages are formed.

The Mongols in Southeast Asia. One of the regions in which such post-villages had to be established was Yunnan. The Mongols managed to spread farther into the southwest than the Chinese ever had, and finally reached the Irrawaddy River in Burma. Marco Polo actually traveled in the region as an adviser to Kublai Khan, the Mongol leader. Polo reported to Kublai Khan that around the Kunming Lakes were many cities and villages with traders and craftspeople. But beyond that was a land of snakes and serpents, quite empty except for an old market town on the old Burma Road.

Polo went on to report that after coming down from the Yunnan Plateau, a traveler would still have to travel for 15 days "through very inaccessible places and through vast jungles teeming with elephants, unicorns, and other wild beasts" before reaching settled country once again. Finally, Polo said, a traveler would come to a great city on the Irrawaddy, which was probably the trading town of Taguang.

The Mongols and Foreigners. Under the Mongols, foreigners were not confined to a single route. The security of all travelers was assured. The great 14th-century Moslem traveler Ibn Battuta had come overland to China all the way from Africa. He described the safety of China:

China is the safest as well as the pleasantest of all the regions on the earth for a traveler. You may travel the whole nine months' journey to which the empire extends without the slightest cause for fear, even if you have treasure in your charge. For at every halting place there is a hostelry [a resting place where it's possible to sleep] superintended by an officer who is posed there with a detachment of horse and foot [soldiers]. Every evening after sunset, or rather at nightfall, this officer visits the inn accompanied by his clerk; he takes down the name of every stranger who is going to pass the night there, seals the list, and then closes the inn door upon them. In the morning he comes again with his clerk, calls everybody by name, and marks them off one by one. He then dispatches along with the travelers a person whose duty it is to escort them to the next station, and to bring back from the officer in charge there a written acknowledgement of the arrival of all....In the inns the traveler finds all needful supplies, especially fowls and geese.

The Ming Dynasty

Expansion—and Withdrawal. In 1358 the Mongols were overthrown by a native Chinese dynasty known as the Ming. The Ming dynasty began their rule by building on Mongol advances and expanding further. They were especially interested in expanding Chinese sea power, and reached as far as Africa and Arabia with their own fleets. Within a few decades the Ming were demanding tribute (payment) from ports around the Indian Ocean.

But after a few decades more, the Ming decided to stop their expansion. They closed the great eastern ports, which Polo and other world travelers had called some of the largest and richest in the world. They confined foreign trade to just the southern port of Nan-hai—and allowed that only grudgingly.

Within the century, Europeans would start arriving in Chinese ports, desperate to trade for eastern goods directly with the Chinese. When European sailors arrived in China, the Ming behaved as if they were under siege. They barred entry to their seaports, and they built the modern version of the Great Wall of China. For centuries there had been some kind of wall protecting China from the north; under the Ming the wall was made higher and stronger, to keep foreigners out.

Roads Under the Ming. Another side effect of China's withdrawal from world affairs was that the road system fell into disrepair. The Burma Road was closed, as that region once more became independent. Annam, which had broken free from the Mongols, was partly restored to the Chinese for a time—but then the coastal strip and the prime port of Chiaoh-chih were lost once again.

The old Ambassador's Road now extended from Nan-hai in the south to Kaifeng and Beijing in the north. But foreigners were still carefully regulated. Foreign envoys in Nan-hai were housed in segregated quarters while word of their presence was sent to Beij-

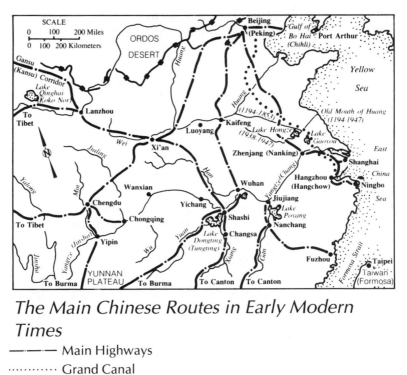

The Main Chinese Routes in Early Modern Times

—·—·— Main Highways

··········· Grand Canal

•—•—•—• Great Wall

ing. Only after they were approved were these visitors then sent north to the imperial court—and then they were able to travel only with official permission and escort. No foreigners were allowed to travel on their own in China, and the Chinese were forbidden to aid any such travelers.

EUROPEANS IN CHINA

The Portuguese Arrive. Despite the difficulties created by the Chinese, the Europeans insisted on establishing trade with them. And they had the military power to back up their wishes.

The first Western Europeans to arrive in China in the modern period were the Portuguese, who came to Nan-hai in 1517. The first contact was not a happy one. They announced their arrival by firing their ship's guns at the city. This did not give the Chinese a very good impression of their peaceful intentions. Later the Portuguese ambassadors were imprisoned and ill-treated, and one of them died in jail.

The Portuguese regained favor by helping the Chinese put down some troublesome coastal pirates. In return, the Chinese allowed them to settle on the peninsula of Macao, downriver from Nan-hai. There they set up a trading post.

Other Europeans. Soon other Europeans made the journey to China, notably the Spanish, the Dutch, and the British. All of them were greeted roughly, though somewhat peaceably. Indeed, some European visitors were given special favor, among them some Jesuit priests who arrived in the late 16th and 17th centuries. These priests were even allowed to found a few missions.

Although the Chinese did not want the Jesuits' to convert them to Christianity, the priests were respected at the Chinese court as scholars. They brought to China word of new discoveries that had been made in the West. This was the first the Chinese had heard of such discoveries as the continents of North and South America and of some startling new inventions, such as guns.

The Europeans and Chinese Roads. Despite the relatively bad state of repair of the Chinese roads, they still compared very well to the European roads of the time. Western visitors were used to rough, rutted tracks that were often muddy or dusty and difficult for carriages to pass over. At the end of the 17th century, French traveler Louis Lecomte wrote the following words of praise:

> One can't imagine what care they [the Chinese] take to make the common Roads convenient for passage. They are fourscore [eighty] foot broad or very near it; the Soil of them is light, and soon dry when it has left off raining. In some Provinces there are on the right and left hand Causeways for the foot Passengers, which are on both sides supported by long rows of trees, and ofttimes terrassed with a wall of eight or ten foot high on each side, to keep Passengers out of the fields. Nevertheless these Walls have breaks, where Roads cross one the other, and they all terminate at some great Town.

Europeans were also impressed with the posthouses and guard stations along the roads, as well as by the trestle-and-balcony construction still to be seen in hilly and mountainous country.

European Dissatisfaction. Nevertheless, China was entering into an ever deeper decline. Europeans were unhappy at being allowed to trade only at Nan-hai, and then only on limited terms. The example of Lord Macartney was typical. In the late 1700s the

Porcelain for the Western markets was transported overland to the main port of Nan-hai. (Anonymous Chinese artist, late 18th century, British Museum)

British sent Lord Macartney to Beijing. They asked the Chinese to let him stay in Beijing as British ambassador. But the Chinese emperor refused. He said that the British, on their "lonely, remote island," were not likely to understand his reasons. But he made it plain that China did not want or need anything British.

Hitherto, all European nations, including your own country's barbarian merchants, have carried on their trade with Our Celestial [Heavenly] Empire at Canton [Nan-hai]. Such has been the procedure for many years, although Our Celestial Empire possesses all things in prolific abundance and lacks no products within its own borders. There was therefore no need to import the manufacture of outside barbarians in exchange for our own produce. But as the tea, silk, and porcelain which the Celestial Empire produces are absolute necessities to European nations and to yourselves, we have permitted, as a signal of favor, that foreign *hongs* [Chinese business associations] be established at Canton, so that your wants might be supplied and your country thus participate in our beneficence.

The Europeans would not stand for this treatment and tried various measures in order to get the kind of trading arrangements

that they wanted. When the Chinese prohibited the import of opium—a dangerous drug from which heroin is made—and some British opium was destroyed at Nan-hai, the British used this as a reason for declaring war on China. The Opium Wars of the 1830s and 1840s were a way for Britain to exert its influence over China.

After these wars, Europeans succeeded in opening trade with Chinese ports other than Nan-hai and, as foreign—especially British—influence spread, the old Ambassador's Road and Burma Road lost their former importance. The roads were so broken up that travelers sometimes made a parallel new road in fields alongside, until the main road was fit to use again.

The British Lord Macartney—shown here meeting with Chinese in Beijing—was one of many ambassadors who tried and then succeeded in opening up China to Western merchants, including opium-sellers. (Authors' archives)

MODERN TIMES

In the 20th century the empire system came to an end in China. Both pressure from the Europeans and internal revolts in favor of democracy weakened the Manchu, China's last dynasty. In 1912 Sun Yat-sen founded the first Chinese republic.

These political changes brought few changes to the old roads of China. The main north–south lines of travel remained as they had for centuries. Even the old trail to Burma still operated.

During World War II the Japanese invaded China and occupied its eastern half. The Burma Road then had a special role to play. The Chinese had to move their capital to the southwest, to Chongqing (Chunking), on the Yangtze River. In an effort to supply the Chinese from the West, the Allies built the famous Burma Road, making use of the old route. However, soon goods were being airlifted into China, rather than being brought in by road, and the Burma Road was allowed to fall into disrepair once again.

In 1949 Communism was established in China as a form of government. Once again the nation shunned contact with the outside world. Today, however, it's possible to take the old trail to Myanmar (Burma) or through the mountains of Sichuan. Those who choose the railroad may well be following the main line of the old Ambassador's Road from Nan-hai to Beijing.

SUGGESTIONS FOR FURTHER READING

Buxton, L. H. Dudley. *China: The Land and the People, A Human Geography* (Oxford: Clarendon Press, 1929). A dated but interesting work on the modern period, with numerous illustrations.

Cameron, Nigel. *Barbarians and Mandarins: Thirteen Centuries of Western Travelers in China* (Chicago: University of Chicago Press, 1976). Reprint of 1970 edition by John Weatherhill, Inc. Despite the subtitle, focuses on Mongol, Ming, and modern travelers, with many excerpts, paraphrases, and illustrations.

Journey Into China (Washington, D.C.: National Geographic Society, 1982). An unusually well-illustrated volume, with a series of articles on themes and regions, along with useful maps.

Lattimore, Owen, and Eleanor Lattimore, eds. *Silks, Spices and Empire: Asia Seen Through the Eyes of Its Discoverers* (New

York: Delacorte Press, 1968). Part of the Great Explorers series. Well-annotated excerpts of Western accounts of Asia.

Morse, Hosea Ballou. *The Trade and Administration of China*, revised edition (Shanghai: Kelly and Walsh, Ltd., 1913). Focuses on the mechanics of trading in the modern period.

Needham, Joseph. *Science and Civilization in China* (Cambridge: University Press, 1965–). An invaluable, multivolume work with extremely useful maps and illustrations, still being published. Volume 1 gives a historical overview of travel, while volume 4, Part 3, includes detailed sections on roads and canals.

Parker, E. H. *China: Her History, Diplomacy, and Commerce, From the Earliest Times to the Present Day*, 2nd edition (London: John Murray, 1917). A detailed early work stressing the modern period.

Polo, Marco. *The Travels* (Harmondsworth, Middlesex: Penguin, 1958). Translated by Ronald Latham. A well-indexed and well-annotated edition of the unabridged text.

Purcell, Victor. *The Chinese in Southeast Asia*, 2nd edition (London: Oxford University Press, 1965). Reviews Chinese presence and influence from early times in each major area, stressing the modern period.

Reischauer, Edwin O., and John K. Fairbank. *East Asia: The Great Tradition* (Boston: Houghton Mifflin, 1958). Volume 1 of *A History of East Asian Civilization*. A good, standard history.

Schafer, Edward H. *The Golden Peaches of Smarkand: A Study of T'ang Exotics* (Berkeley: University of California Press, 1963). An interesting study of the beings and items that traveled through China during the T'ang period.

————. *The Vermilion Bird: T'ang Images of the South* (Berkeley: University of California Press, 1967). A diverse work on the people, flora, and fauna of the coastal regions, including Vietnam.

Schurmann, Franz, and Orville Schell, eds. *Imperial China: The Decline of the Last Dynasty and the Origins of Modern China, the 18th and 19th Centuries* (New York: Random House, 1967). Volume 1 of the China Reader series. Combines excerpts of firsthand accounts with analytical essays.

Tregear, Thomas R. *A Geography of China* (London: University of London Press, 1965). A very useful overview, containing a substantial section on historical geography.

4

THE EURASIAN STEPPE ROUTE AND THE RUSSIAN RIVER ROUTES

THE EURASIAN STEPPE ROUTE: GATEWAY TO EUROPE AND ASIA

The Eurasian Steppe Route has been a central part of much of human history. This route leads for thousands of miles over flat, grassy plains called *steppes*. For tens of thousands of years, different peoples have walked or ridden across this natural pathway as they migrated from one place to another.

The peoples who migrated across the Eurasian Steppe Route are the ancestors of many of today's European peoples. Often these "immigrants" were actually invaders, sweeping down across the steppes to conquer the lands of Central Asia and Eastern Europe. After having conquered any one group or tribe, the vanquished would frequently be ousted and forced to find a new land in which to live, free from attack. In this way, over thousands of years, the peoples of Europe and Central Asia reached the lands they occupy today.

The greatest advantage that the Eurasian Steppe Route had was that it was easy to travel. For a group that wanted to migrate from one place to another by choice, this was a good thing. However, frequently the route was used by invaders sweeping over the steppes, looking for new lands to conquer and control.

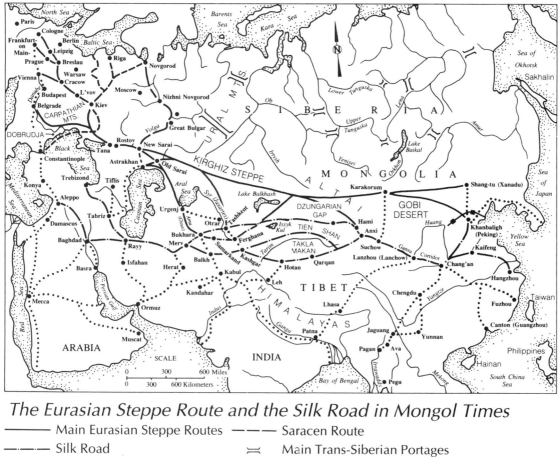

The Eurasian Steppe Route and the Silk Road in Mongol Times

——— Main Eurasian Steppe Routes   — — — Saracen Route

— · — Silk Road   ⚌ Main Trans-Siberian Portages

· · · · · · · · · Main Connecting Routes   •—•—• Great Wall

- - - - - - - Varangian Route   (Beijing)

Thus, the Eurasian Steppe Route was never peaceful enough to become a real trade route. It was more often used as a travel and migration route, and this travel and migration helped shape the faces of Europe and Asia today.

THE GEOGRAPHY OF THE ROUTE

The heart of the Eurasian Steppe Route is the fertile northern steppeland. This lies between the swamps around the Dnieper and Volga rivers (in today's Soviet Union) and the great southern seas of Asia—the Black, the Caspian, and the Aral.

The Eurasian Steppe Route ran from the Ukraine (in today's Soviet Union) eastward south of the Ural Mountains into the vast Kirghiz Steppe of southern Siberia. Going east toward today's country of China, the route passed through the Dzungarian Gap, a wide pathway between the Altai Mountains and the Tien Shan (Celestial Mountains). It then crossed the windswept plateau of today's country of Mongolia, past the Mongolian city of Karakorum. From Karakorum, the route had two branches: one led to Beijing and the other to Shang-tu—Xanadu—just to its north.

To the west, the Eurasian Steppe Route led into Central Europe. Central Europe is somewhat protected by the boomerang-shape Carpathian Mountains. The Eurasian Steppe Route fed into Europe on both sides of these mountains. Two branches of this route led out from the Black Sea. One went northwest, through the city of Lvov (in the Soviet Ukraine) into Poland, and across the northern European plain. This route hooked up with roads to Vienna and Frankfurt. The other way around the Carpathians led southwest from the Black Sea, along the coastal plain of Dobrudja, in today's country of Yugoslavia. From this plain it picked up another trade route, the Orient Route, along the Danube River, which in turn led into the heart of Europe. Frequently in early times invaders would use the Danube River and the Dobrujda to mount attacks toward the Mediterranean.

The Russian River Routes. In medieval times northern Europeans opened up one more connection between Europe and Asia. These were the Russian River Routes. One river route ran from the Baltic to the Black Sea, along the Dnieper River. The other ran from the Baltic to the Caspian Sea, along the Volga River.

In ancient times the Danube River and the Dobrujda, parts of the Eurasian Steppe Route, had been the main routes for invasion. This was because much of European civilization was centered around the Mediterranean. In medieval and modern times, however, the Russian River Routes were more often used, as northern Europe and Russia became more powerful. Both Napoleon and Hitler, for example, used these routes as they moved from northern Europe into Russia.

EARLY TIMES

We know very little about the early peoples who lived on and traveled the steppes. Archaeologists have little evidence to enable

them to study the peoples of the steppes, though burial mounds have offered some clues in detecting how these people lived. Records kept by people who were more culturally advanced tell us something about what they knew of the people of the steppes.

The early peoples of the steppe left behind them huge burial mounds, some over 50 feet high, standing out sharply against the level Eurasian Steppe north of the Black Sea. (19th-century engraving)

Nomads: The Wandering Peoples. The early steppe peoples were most certainly nomads. These wanderers subsisted as hunters and gatherers as they travelled along the Eurasian Steppe looking for food. During their wanderings they passed on new ideas from one people to another all along the route.

This exchange and spread of culture continued for many thousands of years. Gradually humans in different parts of Eurasia developed new ideas and techniques, such as shaping stone into useful tools and making sturdy clay pots. As these new practices sprung up, nomads communicated them along the Eurasian Steppe Route. The peoples of the Near East were the first to adopt a more settled life. They discovered methods of cultivation that enabled them to settle down in one place.

The nomads on the Eurasian Steppe Route, however, did not become farmers. They learned to tame cattle, sheep, horses, and, in dryer areas, goats and camels, and gradually became herders. Thus, they were still wanderers, constantly driving their flocks to new pastures and sources of water.

In about 2500 to 3000 B.C., wheeled vehicles were invented. The first form of transport with wheels were wheeled carts drawn by oxen, asses, or the small horses of those days. These early carts were more useful to farmers than to nomads because the carts were better equipped to travel short distances over fields than long distances over grassy plains.

Then two-wheeled vehicles, in which the animal pulling the chariot was actually carrying part of the weight, were invented. This made it possible to travel more quickly and easily over long distances. The use of this form of vehicle quickly spread across the Eurasian Steppe and soon reached China.

The Eurasian nomads contributed many of their own ideas, as well as passing on the ideas of others. For instance, they were the first people to tame and breed horses so that they could be used to pull carts and carry people. This discovery would be part of a major transformation of life on the steppes.

Peoples of the Steppe. It was not just ideas and customs that changed hands. Different races also evolved as different groups mixed and married. Many of these groups became the ancestors of the modern peoples in Europe and Asia today.

One such people were the ancestors of the Mongols. The Mongols today live in the country of Mongolia, but for many years they were a major power in China and Central Asia. The Mongols were relatively short, dark-haired people with deep-set eyes and un-bearded, yellow-brown skin. Another people were the ancestors of the Turks. Today the Turks live in the country of Turkey, but for many centuries they were rulers of an empire that stretched across the Middle East. The ancestors of the Turkish people were taller, lighter-skinned, and hairier than their neighbors. Finally there were the Indo-Europeans. These were ancestors of the culture that would come to rule most of Europe and West Asia. Their homeland seems to have been north and west of the Black Sea, but by about 2500 B.C., they had expanded westward into Central Europe.

The Indo-European Cultures Expand. Around 2000 B.C. the Indo-Europeans began to move out in all directions. Gradually they broke up into many distinct peoples. These peoples in turn founded many of the ancient cultures that are the roots of modern European and Asian civilizations.

One people was the Iranians. They moved southwest to the Iranian Plateau. Some of their kin went even farther south, into India. In the west, the Hittites swung down the Dobrujda. They passed to the west of the Black Sea until they reached the Aegean Sea and Asia Minor.

The Hittites were soon followed by several waves of Greeks, who eventually settled in Greece. In Western Europe, the Celts (ancestors of today's Irish, among others) conquered many lands, pushing all the way to the Atlantic and eventually to Britain.

Some Indo-Europeans remained north of the Black Sea. These came to be known as Cimmerians. Other Indo-Europeans, the Slavs and the Balts, occupied more northerly parts of Europe.

The Indo-Europeans and Their Horses.

One of the reasons why the Indo-Europeans were able to make so many conquests and be so dominant throughout the Eurasian landmass was their superior ability at raising powerful horses, which could transport them into battle and pull two-wheeled chariots. They also developed a compound bow that could—unlike an ordinary bow and arrow—be shot easily and with power from a fast-moving vehicle. At that time, the

The steppe nomads' large felt tents, called *yurts*, were actually mobile homes pulled by teams of oxen. (By Quinto Cenni, from H. Yule and H. Cordier, *The Book of Ser Marco Polo*, 1903)

combination of superior horsemanship and superior weaponry was unbeatable. Thus, these warrior nomads were able to choose where they traveled, driving other peoples out of their homes.

In their travels, the Indo-Europeans came into contact with people in the Near East who had learned to work with bronze—a mixture of copper and tin that, at that time, was the strongest metal known. Soon the Indo-Europeans carried bronze-working techniques to the East, as they moved in that direction across Central Asia.

The invention of the wheel had revolutionized nomadic life. Every season, nomads moved on to another place that would have more grazing, more water, and a better climate for their herds. They made these trips with long strings of carts, on which they carried all their possessions, including their tents, which were called *yurts*. These were made from wicker frames covered with hides or felt (a fabric of matted animal hair). Sometimes the cart that carried a yurt was so big that its wheels were 20 feet apart.

The nomads of the steppe gradually became accomplished riders and came to wear clothing more suited to their lives. Once nomads wore robes and sandals. Now they wore trousers and boots.

The nomads lived by their herds of cattle, sheep, and goats and used camels, oxen, and asses to haul their heavy goods in slow caravans. But it was the horse that became most important in the steppe nomads' lives. Therefore, each nomad had not just one horse, but as large a herd as could be managed. On military campaigns, each warrior would take a dozen or more horses, so that he could be sure of always having a fresh, well-rested horse.

By the eighth century B.C., the nomads had become skilled at shooting bows and arrows while riding their horses. They could ride bareback at great speed, and they were also able to wheel (turn) sharply, controlling their horses with great precision. They had learned how to surprise and surround their enemies and formed an almost invincible cavalry. War chariots went out of fashion and, on the steppe, were used only for ceremonies. These horse-riding nomads became the terror of Eurasia.

THE HUNS

The Indo-Europeans were not the only significant power on the Eurasian Steppe. In the East the main nomadic power was a group that the Chinese called the Hsiung-nu. Later the Europeans called these people Huns.

The Huns were an ethnically mixed people, part Turk and part Mongol. They were originally located in Central Asia, and they pressed hard on the Chinese. As early as 500 B.C., the Chinese had built a huge wall to repel the Huns. Eventually this wall, built and rebuilt many times, would be known as the Great Wall of China, a huge structure that snakes thousands of miles through the northern part of China.

The Chinese had had to build a wall because the open steppe offered no natural protection from the Huns, either to the north or to the west. When the Huns expanded westward, they pushed many of the Indo-Europeans still farther west. And when the Indo-Europeans moved west, they in turn pushed other peoples out of the way.

The Hsiung-nu in Asia. Despite the defensive wall, the Chinese still felt pressure from the Hsiung-nu. The Hsiung-nu had been forced to seek new lands after their lands had been afflicted by a drought in the first century A.D. They had lost much grazing land during the drought.

In addition to this need for new pasture land, a Mongol group called the Sien-pi began to move out of Manchuria into Hsiung-nu territory in Mongolia.

The result of the Sien-pis' move was like a slow tidal wave sweeping across Eurasia. One group of Hsiung-nu crashed through the Great Wall of China in the second century A.D. They destroyed China's great northern cities and split what was then a unified country into many smaller states. It would take China several more centuries to be reunited once more

The Huns Move West. The Sien-pi pressed the rest of the Hsiung-nu westward. They retreated through the Dzungarian Gap onto the Russian Steppe. As the Hsiung-nu moved west, they took control and mixed with some of the many peoples they found on their way. In the process, they created a new people—the Huns, who would soon strike terror farther west in Europe.

The Huns and Their Horses. The Huns always traveled with great herds of horses—a dozen or more for each warrior—and many cattle for food. To feed these herds, the Huns had to keep on the move, always looking for new grazing land. When pressure from other peoples forced them to move, they could not always keep their herds in good pastures and had to adopt a more primitive hunting-and-gathering life-style in order to survive.

In the first century A.D. while looking for fresh pastures, they forced their way south through the Caucusus Mountains. St. Jerome wrote of them:

> They filled the whole earth with slaughter and panic as they flitted hither and thither on their swift horses. They were at hand everywhere before they were expected. By their speed they outstripped rumor, and they took pity neither upon religion nor rank nor age nor wailing childhood.

The Huns and the Decline of Rome. At this time the greatest power in Europe was the Roman Empire. This mighty empire had grown out of a small city on the banks of the Tiber River in Italy. At its peak, the Roman Empire controlled huge portions of both Europe and Asia and helped shape modern Europe in many ways.

Eventually the Roman Empire split into two parts. The Western Roman Empire, ruling in Europe, adopted Catholicism as its official religion. The Eastern Roman Empire ruled in Asia Minor and the South Balkans, and was centered in the region that today is known as Turkey. This empire followed the Eastern Orthodox Church.

When the Huns and other nomadic peoples began moving westward, the Roman Empire was in decline. The invasions of nomadic peoples from the steppes accelerated this decline. Eventually the Western Roman Empire fell. The Eastern Roman Empire, however, remained strong and became known as the Byzantine Empire.

Attila the Hun. As the Western Roman Empire declined, the Huns became more and more unified and powerful. They were helped to unite by a leader known as Attila. In the fifth century A.D., Attila led a group of Huns through the Roman frontier at Belgrade (the capital of modern Yugoslavia) and swept on into the Balkans (in Eastern Europe). The Huns also moved north into Germany and France.

But there the Huns faced a stalemate. They had made a great two-pronged push into Eastern and Western Europe—and in the process they had lost much of their strength. Meanwhile, the Europeans had had time to develop their own cavalry so that they could effectively fight back.

The Huns were forced to retreat, though they managed to inflict great damage, especially in northern Italy. When Attila died in A.D. 453, the Hun armies collapsed. Most of the Huns went back across the Carpathian Mountains into the heartland of Asia. They settled mostly around the lower Don and Volga rivers, in the part of the world that today is in Russia.

RESETTLEMENTS

The Turks. The Huns were now no longer a major Eurasian power. But in the sixth century, a new power arose on the Eurasian Steppe—the Turks. The Turks were known to the Chinese as the Tu-Chueh. They were of a mixed ethnic background but united by a common language. The original homeland of the Turks was east of the Altai Mountains, on the Orkhon River, south of Lake Baikal (in what today is Mongolia and Soviet Siberia). However, they soon moved westward, closer to the area that is modern Turkey. In these early centuries the Turks were beset by internal strife that curbed their ability to expand. Thus, the eastern part of the Eurasian Steppe Route was relatively peaceful.

Bulgars and Avars. In the West, on the other hand, some offshoots of the Huns continued to attack various places in Europe. A people known as the Bulgars were based on the lower Volga and Don rivers. They mounted several attacks on the Byzantine Empire from this base.

The Turks drove another group of Huns—the Avars—out of Mongolia. The Avars moved westward also. So the Byzantines adopted a dangerous policy. They used the Avars to help defeat the Bulgars.

Some of the Bulgars were driven across the Danube River into the Balkans, to become the ancestors of modern-day Bulgarians. Others were driven north to the Volga River, where they established the trading center of Great Bulgar.

But the Avars, once incited, were not easily stopped. Like Attila before them, they swarmed onto the Hungarian plain, pushing Germanic peoples ahead of them. These resettlements continued as the Avars' attacks went on, for two whole centuries.

Eventually, in the late eighth century, the Avars were driven back across the Carpathian Mountains. But they left an important cultural contribution behind them—the stirrup. The saddle had already been developed. Thus, the basic tackle needed to ride horses was now in place all over Europe.

THE KHAZARS

In a pocket between the Black and Caspian seas, somewhat protected from the waves of steppe invaders, the kingdom of Khazars had developed. The Khazars were another group of mixed origins, but mostly of Turkish background. Before the seventh century, the Khazars had been nomads. But in the seventh century, they adopted the more settled life of traders. They brought goods westward from the steppe across the Black Sea to the Byzantine Empire, their main trading partner.

Many kinds of traders came to the Khazar capital of Itil, at the mouth of the Volga River on the Caspian Sea, in today's Soviet Russia. Itil was a city of many religions: Christians (mainly Eastern Orthodox Greeks from the Byzantine Empire); Jews from the west; and Slavs and Volga Bulgars from the north, who at that time had their own religions. Moslems had also come from the south.

The Khazars themselves eventually became Jews. For many centuries this was the only independent Jewish state in the world.

Except for the region controlled by the Volga Bulgars, areas to the north of Itil were expected to pay tribute to the Khazars. Early stories tell of how "the Khazars came upon [people] as they lived in the hills and forests, and demanded tribute from them," generally "a white squirrel skin drawn from each hearth." The Khazars offered some compensation for the tribute they demanded, however. For centuries they were strong enough to act as something of a barrier against the nomads who were still making raids from the eastern steppe.

THE RIVER ROUTE

The great Russian rivers are easily navigable. They are fairly level and have few rough rapids. They also run fairly close to one another, so it's easy to *portage*, or travel the distance over land between rivers. Thus, the Russian rivers became natural trade routes.

Communities on the River Routes. Many settlements grew up along the Russian rivers, built by people who wanted to take advantage of the trade. After the retreat of the Huns in the fourth century, the Slavs used these rivers to expand in all directions. The Slavs became the ancestors of the people living today in Russia,

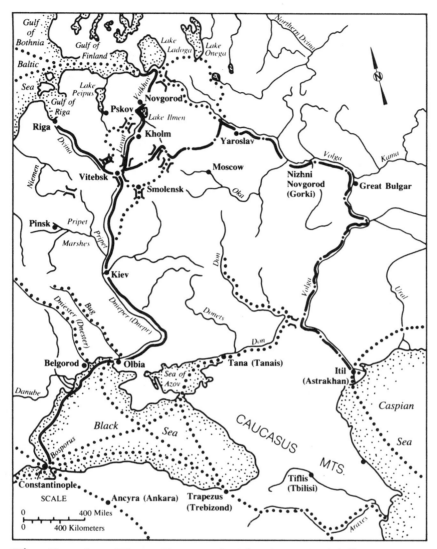

The Russian River Routes in the Late Middle Ages

——— Main Varangian Route

—·—·— Main Saracen Route

·········· Other Connecting Routes

⋈ Main Portages

Poland, the Ukraine, and the Balkans, for that is where they expanded.

Once the river routes were opened, other peoples expanded as well. In the ninth and 10th centuries, there was a great Scandina-

Varangian traders on the Russian River Routes hauled or carried their boats on overland portages. (Det Kongelige Bibliotek, Copenhagen)

vian expansion. As part of that, Swedish Vikings (pirates) known as Varangians moved into the Russian river area. The Byzantines called these Swedes the Rus, which was how the land they moved into acquired the name Russia.

Slaves and Slavs. The Rus conducted trade in furs and slaves. They captured many Slavs and sold them. They sold so many Slavs that the word *slave* eventually came into being. Once the Rus gave up making their raids, they set up trading relations with the Byzantines.

The Dangerous Rivers. Whether in war or in peace, the Rus would gather each spring, as soon as the ice melted on the rivers. Their gathering point was the city of Kiev on the west bank of the Dnieper River. (Today Kiev is the capital of the Soviet Ukraine). From Kiev they would all head south in their dugout canoes. Though the river route was relatively easy all the way south, it did have some dangers. One was the 40-mile-long Dnieper Rapids, on the easternmost curve of the river. A 10th-century Byzantine book called *De Administrando Imperio (How the Empire Must Be Governed)* noted that at the first of these rocky stretches, the river narrows down to the width of a playing field. Then, the book continues,

in the middle there are high and dangerous rocks which stick out like islands. The water rushes up and over them, plunging down the other side with a great and terrifying roar. The Russes do not therefore dare to pass through them; they put in at the bank, landing some of the men, and leaving the goods in the boats; they try out the way with their bare feet lest they strike a rock. While some at the prow and others in the middle do this, those in the stern propel with poles, and so, with the greatest care they get past this first obstruction, keeping in close to the river bank...

The Rus passed many other barriers on this dangerous stretch of river. Many of the men and their human cargo of slaves had to leave the canoes and walk along the bank when the river became too hazardous. Some dragged the boats along the ground; others carried the boats and their supplies on their shoulders.

Once the rapids were passed, the Rus made a sacrifice to their gods to thank them for the safe passage. Then they had to sail another four days until they reached the Black Sea.

At the sea, the Rus turned their canoes into sailing ships by adding masts, sails, and rudders to take advantage of the sea breezes. They sailed around the coast of the Black Sea to the Byzantine capital city of Constantinople (today's city of Istanbul, in Turkey).

Scholars think that the Rus probably left their boats behind in Constantinople, although they don't know how the Rus got home from there. They infer, however, that the Rus probably saved their oars, oarlocks, and other boat fittings, and used them on the new boats that they made the next spring.

The Rus Expand. The Rus tried to expand their trade routes—but in doing so, they made a fatal error. In the late 10th century they conquered the Volga Bulgars and the Khazars. But in doing this, they removed the very states that had acted as buffers to their power base. They were now completely exposed to the nomads of the steppes, who soon moved west quickly.

Pressure had been building from the east for some time. In the previous century a people called the Magyars had been pushed into the Hungarian plain by a people called the Pechenegs.

The Pechenegs gathered strength and influence and now came in full force against both the Rus and the Byzantines. In 968 the Pechenegs laid siege to the city of Kiev itself. Four years later they killed the Grand Prince Svyatoslav, the man who had planned the Russian expansion. Svyatoslav met a particularly gory fate. In an ancient nomadic custom, "the nomads took his head and made a cup out of his skull, overlaying it with gold, and they drank from it."

The Byzantine Empire did not have as much trouble with the Pechenegs as the Russians experienced. The Pechenegs exerted so much influence that they managed to bring the Russian state—and the city of Kiev—into their Eastern Orthodox Christian religion. For many centuries afterwards the people of this region would be members of the Eastern Orthodox Church or of one of its offshoots, the Russian Orthodox Church.

Life for the people of Kiev declined still further in the 11th century, when the city was sacked and its people enslaved by nomadic rulers.

Throughout this period, Western Europe had been reviving its own trading routes. So the Eurasian routes through Russia began to lose their importance, both because of war and because of competition from the west.

THE MONGOLS

Another significant invader from the steppes was the Mongols. Like other invaders, their migrations and invasions resulted in the movement of other peoples, reshuffling the maps of Europe and Asia during the centuries of their power.

History of the Mongols. Originally the Mongols came from Manchuria. Today Manchuria is the northeastern region of the country

Like many other invading nomads, the Magyars headed for the Hungarian plain with all their goods and herds. (Library of Congress)

of China, but many centuries ago it was a separate country north of China. The Mongols were descended from the ancient Sien-pi, who had pushed south and west to the region that is now Mongolia. Sometimes the Mongols were called Tatars, which came from the Chinese word, *ta-ta*, meaning "nomads."

One group of the Mongols was known as the Khitans. In the 10th century they had moved into north China. Under their influence China's capital moved northeast, near the location of the modern capital of Beijing. Over the centuries the Khitans became known as the Khitai. Eventually northern China became known as Khitai —or, to the Europeans, Cathay. (See Chapter 2.)

But it was not until the 13th century that the Mongols of Central Asia achieved their greatest power.

Genghis Khan, Leader of the Mongols. The man responsible for the Mongols' great success was a prince named Temujin, which meant "Iron." When Temujin began winning battles, he took the name "Genghis," which meant "World-Encompassing" or "World-Surrounding." In the early 13th century, Genghis Khan ("Khan" means "leader") held sway at both ends of the Eurasian Steppe

Trading cities like Khiva in Central Asia thrived during the time of the Pax Mongolica—the Mongol Peace —(1260–1368). (From a design by Captain Feodoroff, of the Turkistan Sharpshooters, authors' archives)

Route—at north China and at the Russian area around the Dnieper River.

By 1260 Genghis and his Mongols had made an empire that stretched from the Black Sea to the Pacific Ocean. To the south he held Persia (the country that is now Iran), China, and Burma (now Myanmar). This was by far the largest empire the world had ever seen. For the first—and last—time in human history, it was possible to travel across Eurasia and remain entirely under the rule of one power.

Like other Eurasian nomads, the Mongols had a taste for the finer things produced by the richer peoples around them. Such things could be found at some of the main trading centers along another trade route, the Silk Road. (See Chapter 2.) The Mongols valued the skills of the city-dwellers and often hired or enslaved people to serve them as they traveled, using city folk as scribes (people who wrote things down), metalworkers, and so on.

The raids that they led on the Western Europeans terrorized whole peoples and drove them north and west into mountains and marshes for safety. Still, the Mongols were able to capture large numbers of European slaves. Many of these slaves also were skilled craft workers—goldsmiths, scribes, tentmakers, and others.

These slaves were taken to Karakorum, the Mongol headquarters. After 1264, when the Mongols further expanded their power, European slaves from Hungary, Germany, or Russia could also be found in the Chinese winter capital of Khanbaligh (Beijing) and summer capital of Shang-tu (Xanadu). These captives were probably the first Europeans to have crossed Eurasia to China for several centuries.

During this period the Europeans also began to send ambassadors to the Mongols in the hope of diverting the Mongols' attacks from themselves and on to the Moslems living in the Middle East and northern Africa.

The Mongols did ease their attacks on Europe, for several reasons. One was that when they moved their headquarters east to Khanbaligh, Europe seemed distant to them. They did not want to marshal the resources to make such long attacks. Another reason was that they realized that taxing was more profitable than destruction. If they sacked and destroyed a city, they could no longer profit from it. If they only taxed it, however, they could continue to collect money and goods for years to come.

In a similar vein, they realized that trade was more profitable than destruction. They began to favor the idea of opening a trade route across the Eurasian Steppe, in order to trade with Europe.

THE POLOS

One family did a great deal to establish relations between Europe and Asia—the Polo family. In 1260 two merchants from Venice, Italy, set out into Mongol territory. Their names were Nicolo and Maffeo Polo.

The year 1260 was significant because it marked the beginning of the century of Mongol rule in Asia. That century was one of Asia's most peaceful. Because one power ruled the entire span of Eurasia, it was able to guarantee safe travel from east to west.

The Polo brothers took advantage of this peaceful time. Nicolo and Maffeo went to Bukhara—then Mongol territory, today part of Soviet Kazakhstan. They settled there and traded for three years.

Then the new Khan, Kublai, sent word to the Polos to head east. They went all the way to Khanbaligh, where Kublai Khan quizzed them about Europe. He sent them back to Italy with an interesting request. Because the Mongols were exploring many different religions at this time, Kublai Khan wanted the Catholic Church to send 100 missionary-scholars to China. He wanted them to teach his court about Christianity and argue the merits of their religion with people from other religions. The Catholic Pope sent two missionary-

On their first visit to the Mongol capital, Nicolo and Maffeo Polo—father and uncle of Marco—received a golden tablet from the Great Khan, giving them safe passage across Asia back to Europe. (From *Livre des Merveilles du Monde*, reprinted in H. Yule and H. Cordier, *The Book of Ser Marco Polo*, 1903) scholars. However, they did not complete their journey, and thus the mission was not successful.

Many merchants were interested in going east. The Polos themselves eventually returned, along with Nicolo's son, Marco Polo. They avoided the steppe, however, and traveled mainly by way of the old Silk Road. (See Chapter 2.) All three Polos had been forced into the service of the Mongols and had served the Khan for 17 years before returning to their homeland.

The Polos' Grand Journey. Marco Polo's record of these years stunned Europeans. At this time, Europe was much less developed in general than China. Rough Europeans were shocked to hear of the amazing grandeur of the China of this time.

Polo's description of Khanbaligh was especially surprising to the Europeans. Although the Khan lived there only for the winter months of December, January, and February, the city was quite splendid:

> All around the city there is a first row of walls, square in shape, each side being eight miles long. All along the wall there is a deep ditch, and in the middle of each side a grate through which pass all the people who come to this city. Then there is a space of a mile, where the troops live. Then you come to another square wall, twenty-four miles long....In the middle of these circuits of walls rises the Great Khan's palace, which is the...largest that was ever seen....The inside walls of the halls and rooms are all covered with gold and silver, and on them are painted beautiful pictures of ladies and knights and dragons and beasts and birds and diverse other things. The ceiling is also made in such a way that one sees nothing else on it, but pictures and gold. The great hall is so vast and large that quite six thousand men could banquet there. There are so many rooms as to surpass all belief...The roof is varnished in vermilion [red], green, blue, yellow, and all other colors; and so well and cunningly is this done, that it glitters like crystal, and can be seen shining from a great way off all round.

This was a far cry from nomadic tents—and from the crude European dwellings of the time.

Difficult Crossings. Europeans at first did not believe Marco Polo's stories. But eventually, in the first half of the 14th century, many European merchants made their way across the steppes. This was the heydey of the Eurasian Steppe Route as a great trade route.

This was wagon country. As early as the 13th century, the European traveler William de Rubruck had provided a vivid picture of the nomads' use of wagons. While the male warriors lived on their horses, the women and children drove the great wagons:

> One woman will drive twenty or thirty carts, for the country is flat. They tie together the carts, which are drawn by oxen or camels, one after the other, and the woman will sit on the front one driving the ox while all the others follow in step. If they happen to come on a bad bit of track they loose them and lead them across it one by one. They go at a very slow pace, as a sheep or an ox might walk.

Moslem traveler Ibn Battuta left a record of a different part of east–west travel—the desert area between the Oxus and Jaxartes rivers:

> ...we went on for thirty days by forced marches, halting only for two hours each day, one in the forenoon [morning] and the other at sunset. The length of the half was just as long as the time needed to cook and sup....Everybody eats and sleeps in his wagon while it is actually on the move...It is the custom of travelers in this wilderness to use the utmost speed, because of the scarcity of herbage [grass—what the animals in the caravan needed to eat]. Of the camels that cross [this desert] the majority perish [die] and the remainder are of no use

Once they took China, the Mongols moved their capital eastward along the steppe to this great plain where they built Khanbaligh—the city of the Khan—shown in the distance. (Adapted from Dr. Rennie, *Peking and the Pekingese*, reprinted in H. Yule and H. Cordier, *The Book of Ser Marco Polo*, 1903)

except a year later after they are fattened up. The water in this desert is at certain known water-points, separated by two or three days' march...

No matter which route travelers took, their ultimate destination was always Khanbaligh. Under Mongol rule, these routes were relatively safe and well organized. Along the road travelers met armed Mongolians who were supposed to provide safe conduct for merchants, at a payment of so much per packload. In practice, however, the armed Mongolians often forced travelers to make payments all along the way. And any merchants who died along the road forfeited all their property to the lord of the country, unless someone else in the group could prove he was the dead man's brother.

Despite these dangers, however, merchants and other travelers used the Eurasian Steppe Route frequently. Between 1260 and 1368—the years of Mongol rule—it was a true international highway.

RUSSIAN POWER

During this period the Russians were the unwilling subjects of the Mongols, whose power extended over Russian territory. The Rus, a people descended from Swedish Vikings, had intermarried with the Slavs, to become one people with one language—the Slavonic. Under the pressure of Mongol raids, the Russians had retreated northward into forests and marsh country. There the Mongol nomads would not easily follow them.

Because the farmlands in the south were in nomad hands, the Russians had to find new ways to live. Some went back to a life-style of hunting, fishing, and trapping. Others chose to clear forested land in the north, creating new farmland and extending the steppe.

From Kiev to Novgorod. Kiev, farther south in the Ukraine, never regained its power, for it was too exposed on the steppe. But the city of Novgorod, farther north, in Russia, was well protected. Novgorod was built on an island in the middle of a marsh. It became the main Russian trading center, on the old Varangian trade route that still connected the Baltic with the Black Sea.

The Russians Move East. The Russians could not move south, for they were blocked by the Mongols. At the Volga in the west, they were blocked by the Bulgars. Where then could the Russians expand?

They decided to move east, going along the Oka and upper Volga rivers. By 1147 they had founded the small settlement of Moscow on a tributary of the Oka River. Another city, called Nizhni (Lower) Novgorod, was founded at the junction of the Oka and Volga rivers. The Russians were still weaker than the Mongols, however, and were the victims of many attacks and raids.

The Rise of Moscow and the Volga. Moscow began to become more significant and, by 1367, it had exchanged its old wooden fort—symbol of the medieval Russian city—for the great stone walls of the Kremlin (Citadel, or fortress). With the rise of Moscow, the Volga River became the prime river route to the south. Previously, the Dnieper had been the main route. But the Volga had more connections: it fed into the Caspian Sea and also, with only a short portage to the Don River, into the Black Sea.

During the 13th and 14th centuries, the states of Russia and the Ukraine continued to be under Mongol rule. Russian and Ukrainian princes had to make regular trips eastward to declare loyalty and pay tribute to the Mongol rules. If they did not do this, their lands were ruined and their people enslaved.

The southern states suffered the most. A priest named Brother Carpini made a trip east in 1246. Here is how he described Kiev:

Once a small wooden stockade, Moscow came to be dominated by the great stone fortress called the Kremlin. (From Cornelius de Bruin, *Travels into Muscovy, Persia....*, 1737)

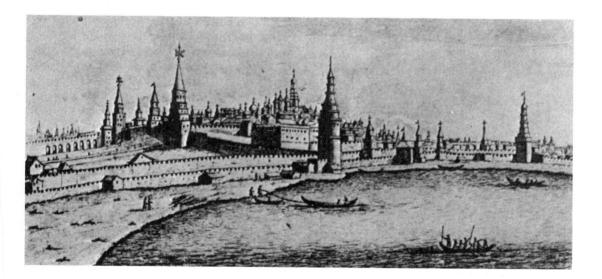

we found an innumerable multitude of dead men's skulls and bones lying upon the earth. For it was a very large and populous city, but it was now in a manner brought to nothing: for there do scarce remain two hundred houses, the inhabitants whereof are kept in extreme bondage.

Travel and trade in Siberia was so crude in this period that the great Moslem traveler Ibn Battuta went no farther than Great Bulgar. He wrote:

One travels in these areas only in small carts which are drawn by strong dogs...Only rich merchants, each of whom takes a hundred vehicles with him are wont [used] to travel in these wastes. The carts are also laden with food, drink, and firewood....In exchange for their own goods they are offered skins of sables, white squirrels, and ermine...Those who travel to these places do not know whether they are demons or men to whom they sell their goods and with whom they trade; for they never see them face to face.

What Ibn Battuta was describing was the ancient practice of silent barter, which has been used throughout the world. In this way people who had no common language could still carry on trade. Each side would make a pile of goods to trade. Then they would add or subtract some goods from their side and watch the person on the other side do the same. Eventually, without words, they would come to an agreement about what to trade.

The End of Mongol Rule. By the end of the 14th century, the great days of the Mongols were passing. As the Mongol confederation fell apart, Russia became free to expand.

But with the end of the Mongols came also the end of caravans on the Eurasian Steppe Route. Trade would continue, but not between nations as before. Now trade was generally practiced in trading chains among the nomads themselves.

Travel on the route was no longer safe for Europeans. Nevertheless, through the 14th century, goods continued to make their way by various routes to the Caspian and Black seas, where Italian traders came to pick them up. In the 15th century, caravans of as many as 800 camels were still reported in Samarkand, headed for the western seaports.

Then, in 1453, the Turks captured Constantinople, the capital of the Byzantine Empire. This event changed the geography and politics of the Middle East. Now the Turks ruled the Ottoman

Empire (a vast state founded by Ottoman Turks in the late 13th century) from Constantinople, replacing the official Eastern Orthodox Christianity with their Moslem religion. Moslems and Christians did not get along during this period, at last partly because the Moslem Turks and the Christian Europeans were fighting for control over east–west trade. As a result, Europeans turned their attention to the sea routes that would take them east, so that they did not have to use the land routes that were controlled by the Turkish Moslems.

On the Russo-Chinese border, traders met to exchange tea for furs and other specialty goods. (By Thomas Witlam Atkinson, from *Travels in the Regions of the Upper and Lower Amoor...*, 1860)

Exploring Siberia. By the middle of the 15th century, the Eurasian Steppe Route was no longer a major international trade artery. But a new route was developing in the East. Over the centuries, the Russians had gradually drifted across the low Ural Mountains into the forests of Siberia, hunting for furs. At this time Siberia was occupied by many native peoples, similar to the Native Americans and Inuits (Eskimos) living in North America.

The Russians used Siberia as a land for trapping and trading, and Russian traders developed a complex series of portages so that they could go mostly by water along the vast network of Siberian rivers. By the end of the 17th century, they had reached past Siberia's huge Lake Baikal all the way to the Pacific Ocean.

Chinese Expansion. During this period the Chinese had thrown off the rule of the Mongols and established the Ming dynasty. The Ming did not like foreigners, but they did like trade, which continued under their rule. After the Ming dynasty came the Manchu, China's last dynasty. The Manchu expanded trade and the borders of China itself. By the end of the 18th century, the Chinese controlled the whole eastern half of the Eurasian Steppe.

Trade Routes Between the Giants. Between these two giants—Russia and China—a new trade route developed. Part of the incentive for this development was that the Russians had acquired a taste for Chinese tea. The fastest way to trade in Chinese tea was overland, rather than around three continents by sea. And the Chinese, for their part, were eager for Russian furs. As a result, Russian and Chinese traders met at the border market of Kiachta on a river south of Lake Baikal.

But Chinese and Russian traders had to develop their own new overland trade routes, for the Eurasian Steppe Route was not available. It was under the control of the Cossacks, a wild people who had once been slaves of the Russian empire. When they escaped to the east, they became "free warriors" who made raids in all directions. So Russian traders avoided the steppes and instead took a Trans-Siberian pathway through the Ural Mountains.

Eventually, in the 20th century, the building of a railroad transformed the Trans-Siberian Route into an all-season pathway. The Trans-Siberian Railroad crosses Siberia and links with China and Mongolia.

Modern technology has also changed the Russian river routes. A network of canals replaced the old system of portages, so that larger ships—too big to be portaged—do not have to be lifted out of the water. These canals link the major cities of European Russia with each other and with the nearby seas.

In modern times the European Steppe Route is not an international highway, for politics divides the countries that surround it. Instead, the Trans-Siberian route takes some travelers and trade goods overland across Eurasia. The rest travel by air or sea.

SUGGESTIONS FOR FURTHER READING

Adams, Arthur E., Ian M. Matley, and William O. McCagg. *An Atlas of Russian and East European History* (New York: Praeger, 1966). A useful work with general maps and text commentary.

Grousset, René. *The Empire of the Steppes: A History of Central Asia* (New Brunswick, N. J.: Rutgers University Press, 1970). Translated from the French by Naomi Walford. A full political history, focusing on the Mongol period.

Hudson, G. F. *Europe and China: A Survey of Their Relations from the Earliest Times to 1800* (Boston: Beacon Press, 1961). Reprint of the 1931 edition. An extremely useful review of the main land and sea connections through history.

Lattimore, Owen, and Eleanor Lattimore, eds. *Silks, Spices and Empire: Asia Seen Through the Eyes of Its Discoverers* (New York: Delacorte, 1968). Part of the Great Explorers series. A well-annotated collection of excerpts of classical and modern firsthand accounts.

Legg, Stuart. *The Heartland* (New York: Farrar, Straus & Giroux, 1970). A well-written chronicle of Central Asia from the Indo-Europeans to the Mongols.

Mitchell, Mairin. *Maritime History of Russia, 848–1948* (London: Sidgwick and Jackson, 1949). A fascinating work that includes an excellent treatment of the Russian river routes.

Parker, W. H. *An Historical Geography of Russia* (Chicago: Aldine, 1968). An extremely useful book, with many interesting quotations from firsthand accounts.

Severin, Timothy. *The Oriental Adventure: Explorers of the East* (Boston: Little, Brown, 1976). Tells the stories of many European adventurers and missionaries in Asia in modern times.

Spuler, Bertold. *History of the Mongols: Based on Eastern and Western Accounts of the Thirteenth and Fourteenth Centuries* (Berkeley: University of California Press, 1972). Translated from the German by Helga and Stuart Drummond. A fascinating compilation.

Teggart, Frederick J. *Rome and China: A Study of Correlations in Historical Events* (Berkeley: University of California Press, 1939). A masterly summary of related events on the Eurasian Steppe in the first centuries B.C. and A.D.

INDEX

Dunhuang (city) 36, 44
Dzungarian Gap 78, 83

E

Eastern Orthodox Church 21, 29, 31, 84, 90, 99
Ecbatana (city) 5
Egypt 19
Euphrates River 13
Eurasian Steppe 19, 33, 38–39, 45
Eurasian Steppe Route
    Avars and 85
    Bulgars and 85
    Caravans and 98
    Chinese control of 100
    Genghis Khan and 91–92
    Geography of 77–78
    Huns and 82–85
    Introduction 76–77
    Khazars and 86
    Map of 77
    Peoples of 80
    Turks and 85
    Wagons and 94–96
Explorers and Exploration
    of Central Asia 7–8
    Chang Ch'ien 8–11, 60–61
    Columbus 44
    Ibn Battuta 41, 68, 95, 98
    of India 60–61
    Italian states and 38
    Marco Polo 1, 39–44, 67–68, 94
    of Siberia 100
    of Silk Road 1

F

Fa-Hsien 23
Feathers 55
Ferghana Horses—*See Horses*
Five Foot Way 61
Floods 51
Forts 13

France 45–46, 84
Frankfurt (city) 78
Fur Trade 19, 88, 100

G

Ganges River 54
Gansu Corridor 4
Genghis Khan 38–39, 91–92
Genoa (city-state) 38
Germany 46, 84
Gnosticism 30
Gobi Desert 4
Gold
    China trade 19, 53
    Silk Road and 1, 6
    Spice Route and 61–62
Golden Rule—*See Confucian Golden Rule*
Goldsmiths 92
Grand Canal *66*
Grand Road 5, 54
Great Britain
    Central Asia and 45–46
    China and 45–46, 71–73
    Opium Wars 73
Great Desert Route 18
Great Wall of China 2, 4, 8, 35, 45, *47*, 69, 83
Greeks 81
Guangzhou (city) 54
Gulf of Bo Hai 8, 35
Gulf of Tonkin 54

H

Han Dynasty 21, 59–63
Hangzhou (city) 66
Himalayan Mountains 20
Hindu Kush Mountains 25, 38
Hitler, Adolf 78
Hittites 81
Holland—*See Netherlands*
Horses
    Caravans of 17
    Chang Ch'ien and 9